BILLY CASPER'S
"MY MILLION-DOLLAR SHOTS"

BILLY CASPER'S
"MY MILLION-DOLLAR SHOTS"

By Billy Casper

GROSSET & DUNLAP
A NATIONAL GENERAL COMPANY
PUBLISHERS • NEW YORK

PHOTO OF BILLY CASPER BY JARON SUMMERS

COPYRIGHT © 1967, 1968, 1969 BY NATIONAL NEWS-
PAPER SYNDICATE, INC.
COPYRIGHT © 1970 BY BILLY CASPER ENTERPRISES, INC.
ALL RIGHTS RESERVED
LIBRARY OF CONGRESS CATALOG CARD NUMBER:
74-106311
PUBLISHED SIMULTANEOUSLY IN CANADA

PRINTED IN THE UNITED STATES OF AMERICA

Contents

Introduction · *9*
The Grip · *41*
The Stance · *55*
The Swing · *67*
   The Backswing · 86
   The Downswing · 96
Fairway Shots · *129*
Around the Green · *171*
   Shooting Out of the Sand · 190
On the Green · *201*

ACKNOWLEDGMENT

One of the great satisfactions of the touring pro —as well as the teaching pro—is that his technique or example may help a fellow golfer solve some of his problems. I am deeply indebted to all of the golfers who have encouraged me throughout my career, and I hope this book in some small way will repay them for their attention and loyalty.

Every touring golfer is in a sense a one-man conglomerate. He is constantly in demand for everything but golf—endorsements, exhibits, television appearances and assorted business diversions. I literally made a million-dollar shot two years ago when I placed such interests in the hands of Uni-Managers Incorporated in Los Angeles, headed by a long-time friend, Edward Barner. Without his help, I would never have been able to sustain my playing concentration over the demanding tournament seasons.

Also, without Ed, this book would have been much more laborious in the making.

BILLY CASPER'S
"MY MILLION-DOLLAR SHOTS"

Introduction

Golf is the greatest game in the world. It is frustrating. It is rewarding. It is humbling. It is humiliating. It is exhilarating. It can send you into the depths of despair. It can rocket you into an orbit of incomparable satisfaction and joy. It teaches. It puts a man's character to the anvil and his richest qualities—patience, poise, restraint—to the flame.

I think I shall never forget June 19, 1966. It was the day I learned the value of restraint.

All sorts of thoughts and temptations were reeling through my head as I teed up the ball on the sixteenth hole in the final round of the U. S. Open Championship at the Olympic Club.

Moments before, I had been a hopelessly beaten man. Paired with Arnold Palmer as the tournament leading twosome, I had fallen seven shots back with only nine holes to play. My only hope at that stage appeared to be to avoid complete disgrace.

Suddenly the match took a dramatic and unbelievable turn. A snakey putt dropped for me on the thirteenth green. At the fifteenth, Palmer bogeyed and I birdied. Now I found myself only three strokes back with three to play. For the first time since Arnold had smothered me with an outgoing 33, I felt I had a chance not just to finish respectably but to win.

Then came the sixteenth, and my honor.

The sixteenth at Olympic is a 604-yard, par five dogleg left that gives the impression of being in another county. My first impulse was that perhaps I should take a jet.

I had a tingling sensation as I teed up the ball. Now I have Palmer reeling, I said to myself, I should now give him the knockout punch. I must not let him regain the initiative.

I looked down the long, narrow canyon and the statuesque trees at the left guarding the shortest approach to the green. "Go for it!" an inner voice counselled. "This is no time to be chicken—let 'er out," urged another voice.

Tension gripped me. Opposite forces battled within me and I could feel them churning. I stepped away from the ball momentarily and took a deep breath. It was just time enough for better judgment to gain control. "Don't change tactics now. Be calm. Play within yourself."

The swing felt good as it went back slowly, reached the desired arc and swept through the ball. It wasn't a tremendously long drive but it was straight down the fairway. I let out a relieved breath when it came to the end of its roll.

Palmer stepped to the tee. He is strong and bold. For a decade he had thrilled golf fans with his ability to grab a course by the throat and virtually shake it to death. Palmer lashes into the ball with such explosive force that he almost falls off the tee after his follow-through. The word "caution" is not in his vocabulary.

His long lead diminishing and his seemingly certain title now threatened, Arnold felt this was no time for conservatism. With mighty shoulders and arms like those of a blacksmith, he tore into the ball savagely. There was a resounding thunderclap as the club head struck the ball, a wild cheer from the gallery and then a groan. One hundred and eighty yards from the tee, the ball struck a tree and fell limply into Olympic's wiry rough.

Palmer, certainly one of golf's great competitors of all time, was only warming up to the fight. He took a three-iron and waded into the ball. The ball failed to make the fairway. A third shot was necessary to put the ball back into play and a fourth, a desperate wood, sent it flying into a sand trap.

From my fairway position, I was still a long distance from the green. A fairway wood was dictated. Having viewed Arnie's troubles, I decided this was no time to be a hero. I pulled a two-iron from the bag and hit my second shot down the fairway, leaving me still a middle iron to the green. I could have gained greater distance with a wood but I might have discovered greater trouble.

With a five-iron, I pitched my third shot to the green, thirteen feet from the cup. I sank the putt for a birdie. Arnie got down in two from the bunker for a bogey six. His lead was cut to a single stroke.

It is rather common knowledge among followers of the game what happened after that. Arnold and I tied for the title with 278. In the eighteen-hole playoff the next day, Arnie again shot a 33 on the front nine for a two-stroke lead. But the match suddenly reversed itself—as it had the day before—and I finished with a 69 while Palmer shot 73.

I often wonder what the result might have been had I given way to my first impulse and ambition on the sixteenth hole of that final round at Olympic.

Easy Does It

My advice to anyone wishing to play golf both to enjoy it and win would be this: Don't try to kill the ball. Relax. Swing easy. Play the percentages. Play well within yourself. Play it safe—and score better.

It is a natural tendency to want to slug the ball. The average golfer watches the tournament pros and wants to emulate them. There is a vicarious thrill in feeling the club head smash solidly against the ball and watching the ball form a long, beautiful arc as it reaches out for the fairway.

Yet this can be a rare and temporary thrill and one that is dulled by the aggravation of having to fight your way out of a clump of trees or dig the ball out of tenacious rough, which is more often the case for the bold and reckless slammer. By far the greater satisfaction comes from scoring a birdie or a par on a difficult hole—no matter the method—and going to the locker room with a card that you can brag about to your fellow slaves of the sport.

I used to swing very hard. Now I find that I normally swing with about 80 or 85 per cent of my potential. There are exceptions, of course. Sometimes on a long par four or a par five which can be reached in two, I may find it advisable at the time to let out all the way on a tee shot in order to set up an easier second shot. Generally, it is more expedient to use a relaxed swing. It is defeating to try to hit a seven-iron 170 yards when the task can be accomplished more simply by employing a longer iron and an easier stroke.

The Thinking Man's Game

It was the great Bob Jones who once said that golf is a game played on a five-inch course—the distance between the ears. Ben

Hogan expressed the same philosophy in a more direct if less colorful fashion. He said golf is 30 per cent physical and 70 per cent mental. I agree wholeheartedly with them both.

Golf is—or at least, to my mind, should be—a game of management. It is a thinking man's game, not a hitter's game. The premium should not be on power but rather on shot placement, accuracy, judgment and finesse.

I am distressed that the modern trend of golf course architects is on length rather than subtlety. Why must we have monsters of 7,000 yards and more that tax every ounce of muscle in a golfer's body while putting minimum strain on his brain-power? The tournament pros, with increasing emphasis on brute strength, may struggle through a round over one of these awesome heavyweights with their pride unscathed, but pity the poor average player. He is constantly fighting bogeys and double bogeys and fails to derive the pleasure for which the game is designed.

Golf should be fun. Certainly, it is at times frustrating. The ball is small—only 1.6 inches in diameter. The golfer is forced to strike it with an implement which a wry old Scotsman once said was ill-equipped for the purpose. He is playing against natural physical instincts. Golf is a left-handed game played by right-handers, vice versa in the case of left-handers.

A right-handed person finds he is using his right hand contradictory to its normal function. The left hand, the left side, the left hip are doing the work and the right hand is merely a guiding fork.

Some of the best golfers have been converted left-handers. Ben Hogan is one. Phil Rodgers is another. Bob Charles, the New Zealander who has been the most successful of left-handed golfers, does everything else right-handed.

I mention this to emphasize that golf is one of the toughest of all games to play. In football, baseball, tennis and other sports, you have automatic reflexes working for you. There is a moving object, a moving opponent. You react instinctively. In golf, there is no instinctive reaction, no reflexes.

You are hitting a stationary object toward some fixed target. Sam Snead and Ted Williams, two old fishing buddies, have been debating for years the relative difficulties of hitting a stationary golf ball and a speeding baseball. Williams, the former Boston Red Sox slugger, insists that it's harder to hit a baseball coming at you at perhaps 100 miles per hour. "Maybe so," concedes Snead, "but if you hit a foul ball in golf you have to play it."

Standing over a golf ball on the tee, the golfer may have a hundred messages flashing through his mind: "Watch out for that trap on the right." "Keep the head down." "Keep your eye on the ball." "Keep the left arm stiff." "Don't forget to cock the wrists at the top of the back swing." And on and on *ad infinitum.*

Of course, the brain can transmit only one message at a time to the working parts of the body. Therefore, it is impossible to receive all of these messages and execute them properly. Golf is a game of habit. It is a game of touch and feel. Consistency is what counts.

The goal of the tournament golfer—and it should be the goal of the average golfer as well—is to cultivate a swing that can be repeated over and over again without flaw. This requires a great deal of practice. It also requires concentration.

Fundamentals

The purpose of this book is to set forth a few fundamentals and describe shots as I have played them en route to the million-dollar mark in tournament winnings. The golfer should not necessarily try to duplicate my techniques. Instead, he should evaluate his own game and needs and adapt the hints in this book to them.

There are certain basics it is wise for all golfers to adhere to. These involve the grip, the stance and the fundamental part of the swing, all of which have been refined down through the years. That doesn't mean anyone should copy my exact method of bringing the club back and striking the ball.

What works for one player does not always work for another. For example, I slide my right foot when I swing the club. This helps me. It wouldn't necessarily help someone else. Doug Sanders has a very short, quick swing—cultivated in his youth—which gives the impression that he's punching the ball. Jack Nicklaus seems to leave the ground when he throws all of his power into a drive. Gene Littler's swing is so compact and grooved that it seems it could never develop a kink. There are other top golfers who create long, loose arcs and even some who may make a half-dozen mistakes bringing the club back and correct them all coming down.

Characteristics differ with the individual in the swing except when the club reaches the hitting area. That is the area from the waist into the ball. Some teachers restrict it even more—to the four inches before and after impact. This is the point where both the power and the accuracy of the shot are generated. There can be no variance here.

Once the golfer has found the swing that is the most comfortable and rewarding for him, then his next step is to practice it until it becomes second nature to him. While golf is a thinking game, there is no time to think once you take a stance over the ball. There you must rely strictly on instinct.

Being able to strike the ball solidly and

watch it fly toward the appointed target provides the game's premier thrill. This is where the satisfaction comes. This is the purpose of the game.

"For This Relief, Much Thanks"

Golf should be a form of relaxation, a diversion. If it should take another form—if the player gets tense and edgy, if he cultivates a headache or an ulcer and if his frustrations throw him into fits of uncontrollable temper—then I would suggest that he take up another and less abrasive pastime. Golf is intended to be an outlet, a release of taut emotions.

Happily, for most people it is. For the businessman, it is a relief from dull office routine and commuting problems. For the laborer, golf affords an opportunity to use his muscles in a different way. For both, the game offers diversion. It can require intense concentration. It can be demanding and frustrating, yet at the end of the round the player feels relaxed and stimulated.

As a tournament golfer, playing week in and week out, the game sometimes has an opposite effect on me. I become tired and stale from using my mind and muscles the same way day after day. I find my diversion in fishing or playing billiards. I am still using my mind, my muscles and skills, but in a different way. So fishing and billiards, which like golf require feel, become a form of relaxation. After a while, I return to golf fully refreshed.

Jack Nicklaus and Julius Boros also find relaxation from the tour in fishing. Gary Player prefers to jet to his ranch in Johannesburg where he can romp with his family and horses. Lee Trevino knocks off with his old buddies around El Paso. Arnold Palmer takes to the skies in his jet airplane. Arnie loves to pilot the plane. I am sure this is his private antidote to too much tournament golf.

Golf is more than a form of recreation. It is therapy. And it serves as a gauge for determining the character of men. I can learn more about a person in four hours on the golf course than sitting with him for days in a private office. Golf tests a man's mettle. It reflects his temperament. It reveals his ability to relate to other people and challenging situations. It proves whether he can face and overcome obstacles or let these obstacles overwhelm him.

I am sure that many a multi-million-dollar deal has been finalized either on the course or in the locker room after a round of golf. This also is where qualities of leadership are discovered and rewarded.

Once during a very close and hotly contested presidential campaign, Jimmy Demaret suggested—half in jest and half seriously, I think—that the ideal way to select the nation's chief executive would be to toss all the candidates onto a golf course for an afternoon. "There is nothing like a round of golf to bring out the best and worst in a man," Jimmy said. "A man who can look at a string of bogeys and maintain his poise can run a country."

Uniquely, some of them actually have. Dwight D. Eisenhower perhaps was the most avid of golfing presidents. When the affairs of state weighed heavy on his shoulders, he often would don a pair of dungarees, a battered old cloth hat and chase out to the golf course, surrounded by a cordon of G-men. Once with a club in his hands, he put himself in an imaginary isolation booth and shut himself off from the cares of his office. He played the game with a rare vigor and gusto. He returned and dug into his presidential responsibilities with refreshed enthusiasm.

John F. Kennedy could have been an excellent golfer but was bothered by a hip ailment. Nevertheless, while in office, he played a quick nine holes frequently between appointments. Lyndon Johnson also played, but mainly for outdoor exposure and exercise. Richard Nixon took up the game but acknowledged that he was more of a spectator than a competitive sportsman.

It is a game played by presidents and kings, bricklayers and boot-blacks, and there must be some deep-down comfort in the fact that, once they tee up the ball, they are all equal. Golf plays no favorites. The grass on the putting surface breaks the same way for a monarch as for a mechanic. Sand bunkers are just as hungry for a wayward shot hit by royalty as one flubbed by a pauper.

And if they're to succeed, they all must grip the club alike.

My Philosophy

In this particular section, I am more concerned with imparting my philosophy of golf, hoping that some of the lessons that I have learned in 16 years as a touring professional may be passed on to you. My hope is to make you not only a better golfer but one who finds greater relaxation and pleasure in the game.

I began playing when I was 4½ years old. I took six lessons when I was a junior in high school and they are the only formal lessons I ever had. I used a baseball grip at the time. The rest of my game I worked out on my own. I studied my physical characteristics, tried to adapt the game to them and then set out—through unending practice, study and self-analysis—to build a golf game.

I don't recommend this to the average golfer. My suggestion is, by all means and if possible, go to a professional. Learn the fundamentals of the game, then work, practice and play.

As a youngster, I played in the junior golf program but always was overshadowed by Gene Littler, who was a year older and who grew up in the same San Diego area as I did. Gene and Mike Souchak were the modern Gold Dust Twins, winning almost every tournament in sight, when I turned professional in April, 1954. I was still in the U. S. Navy at the time, not to be discharged until June, 1955.

I recall that Paul Runyan, a former tour player who was one of California's leading teachers, and others shook their heads in wonder when I made the move. I had a terrible grip. I had a quick swing. I was always trying to murder the ball. When I teed the ball up, people didn't know where to stand to be safe. Also, I was hot tempered and had a very cranky disposition.

"You'll never make it, kid," Runyan said. I think he actually was being charitable. He didn't want to see me starving on the tour while he thought I might have made a good living as an insurance salesman or a bank teller. My critics reckoned without what I since have labelled by four Ds—Desire, Determination, Dedication and Discipline. I would recommend this four-point formula to anyone.

I perfected my grip. I strengthened my

left hand. I opened my stance. I took an entirely new approach to the game.

While I never have patterned my game after any other player, I always have had the utmost admiration for Hogan's tournament psychology. He never tried to beat a course to death with sledgehammer blows. He was like a matador teasing an angry bull. He dissected it like a talented surgeon.

I recall that when Ben was the king of golf in the early 1950s, he was a stylist rather than a hitter. He never tried to overwhelm a golf course with sheer power. He was what he liked to refer to as a shot manager. He mentally charted a course and positioned every shot. They said he was so accurate that he played out of his own divots in the fairway as each round progressed.

Hogan played the percentages. I try to do likewise. I feel it is good advice to the average player. First, I feel it is necessary to form a mental image or a picture of the shot you are about to execute. Then you must take into consideration all the factors that could influence the shot—that is, the wind, placement of the flag and surface conditions. Then you must give yourself a margin for error.

It is the natural tendency of golfers to try to shave doglegs, fly the ball over fairway traps or go for the flag when the cup is tucked into a corner of the green behind a necklace of traps. This is suicide. Even the top tournament golfers with supreme confidence in their games rarely take such risks—and then only when a title or a big purse may hinge on the single shot.

In my career, I have taken many chances. Usually it is in a desperate situation where a go-for-broke shot is dictated. Normally when I do it, it is when I know my capabilities. I make sure the percentages are in my favor.

A common failing is the inclination to swing too quickly and swing too hard. It is a disease that infects the tournament player as well as the week-end golfer. Impatience is a deterrent. In anticipation of hitting a good shot, I frequently get overeager and excited. The result is that I swing too quickly. In those circumstances, I am more apt than not to miss the shot.

It is like a hunter on his first foray. He has never killed an animal, but he keeps his gun pointed and ready. Suddenly a deer darts out of the bushes. The hunter becomes so excited, he shoots straight into the air.

This brings us back to our original precept: Don't hurry the shot. Don't try for a little extra. Swing easy. Remember rhythm is the key. Rhythm gets the job done.

Many golfers, having flubbed one shot, will attempt to make up for it on the next one, trying to pull off a recovery that a touring professional would hesitate even to think about. This is a foolish reaction. The intelligent golfer shrugs off the bad shot as a natural error. Instead of compounding the error, he plays the percentages and gets the ball back into play. Many times in a major tournament I have used a five-iron or six-iron to get out of the thick rough when I might have gambled to go for the green with a longer iron or a wood. In the long run, such gambles do not pay.

When I am faced with two fairway traps so close together that it would take a siege gun to go between them, and so far from the tee that only a super drive could send the ball over them, I normally elect to play safe, short of the bunkers. I have a longer second shot but, by playing percentages, I have avoided a hazard that could cost one or two extra strokes.

If the pin is on the left side of the green guarded by a trap and your ball is lying on the left side of the fairway, you should not try to put your approach on the flag. Intelligent management dictates that you should go for the fat part of the green and take a chance on getting down with a longer putt.

There are sound reasons for this conservative strategy, a trademark of Hogan throughout his remarkable career. Faced with a daring and difficult shot, you naturally become tense and apprehensive. Doubt inhibits the swing. Odds on pulling off the shot immediately lengthen. In taking the alternative, your confidence will be stronger and your swing undoubtedly smoother.

The Three "Ts"

Once the golfer has mastered the grip and the swing—and this is rudimentary—then the game becomes one of practice, touch and feel. I refer to them as the three "Ts"—Tempo, Touch and Thinking.

All three are linked to one important chain which we might refer to as concentration.

I realize that it must sound contradictory to speak of relaxation and concentration in the same breath. If you're concentrating, how can you relax? If you're having to think about all the things you are supposed to do, how can you be calm and serene? It seems such thoughts must drive you up the wall.

That is not true at all. It is possible to concentrate and still remain cool. In fact, that's part of true concentration. You must keep telling yourself: "You blew that shot, but don't let it get your goat." "Forget the last hole. You can make it up later." "So the crowd is noisy. Forget it. Keep your mind on the game."

Golf—particularly big-time tournament golf—can have its distractions. As one pundit said, golf is the only sport in the world where the spectators can walk out to the pitcher's box and talk to the pitcher. That is true. The crowd is always at your elbow. Someone is always wanting to chat and give advice.

Friends have often told me that I appear grim on the golf course. They don't understand why I don't smile, wave, joke and laugh it up as do some of the more colorful performers. I don't like to appear to be an old grouch. But I agree with words uttered not long ago by Frank Beard, who was the tour's leading money winner in 1969. "Golf is a business with me," Frank said. "It's like going to the office from nine to five. It's my livelihood. When I'm at my office—on the course—I like to apply myself to my work. When I fail to do this, I think I'm cheating myself out of money."

I agree. Intense concentration is a vital part of golf. When you stand over a ball, you must think of what you are going to do with it. Between shots, you are evaluating conditions—the wind, your next shot, your position in the field. I think concentration is just as vital to the average golfer. Don't worry about a bad shot. Determine to make it up. Put yourself in an invisible isolation booth and forget all the distractions around you.

Practice May Not Make Perfect

Although I worked hard in my early years as a touring pro, I do not practice as much as some golfers, notably Ben Hogan and Arnold Palmer, who have been known to spend hours on the practice tee. I usually hit 75 to 100 balls before a tournament round but this is more a warmup than a practice session. I start with my short irons and work up to the driver, going back to the middle irons before moving over to the practice green for about fifteen minutes of putting before reporting to the first tee.

My reasoning is simple and what is best for me is not necessarily good for the next man. I know my capabilities. I am conscious of my physical and mental needs before a round. I feel if I hit balls for hours in practice it would dull my playing edge.

Also, I never take my golf problems home with me. When I've played a round—good, bad or indifferent—I try not to fret over it. I forget it until the next day. I enjoy being with my family. I enjoy church work. Both give me a great serenity, enabling me to shrug off any golf course frustrations that might develop.

I recommend this to the average golfer. I also recommend a warmup before going to the tee. Never go to the tee cold. One ideal way is to practice chipping and putting while your foursome is being organized or is waiting for the starter's signal. Try different kinds of chip shots from various lies and distances. You will be surprised how many strokes it will save you.

Personally, when I am near a green I like to get the ball up fast. So I chip and run shots rather than punch them at the flag with a minimum of roll and bite. But this is a choice that the individual must make. He must play the shot which he executes best and in which he has the most confidence.

I am frequently asked if I ever lose the groove of my swing and if I ever become stale and lose my rhythm and feel. The answer on both counts is "yes."

All of us—and I am including the touring pros—lapse into bad habits without realizing it. Suddenly we wake up one morning and find that our swing has developed a flaw. It came by degrees and so gradually that it escaped our notice. Then it becomes very difficult to correct. You must jump back to the other end of the pendulum and almost start from scratch again.

I recall the case of Gene Littler. His swing was so compact and so flawless that teachers said there was no way for it to lose its groove. Yet in the late 1950s, after a very successful career, Gene had trouble making the cut. His swing had gone sour. "How do I know how to correct it?" Littler lamented at the time. "I always just put the ball down and hit it and never knew the mechanics of my swing. If I didn't know what I was doing right, how can I know what I am doing wrong?" Fortunately, he found the answer, won the U. S. Open title after that, and again became one of the circuit's top money winners.

Health Means Wealth

You cannot play well if you do not feel well. Therefore, health is very important. It is particularly important to those golfers like myself for whom the game is a livelihood. Golf is a matter of decisions. These decisions come easier if you are alert, fresh, with the mind clear.

My spring campaign, leading up to the Masters, is handicapped because I am allergic to the sprays which are put on Florida courses. So I often am forced to pass up the Florida swing completely. Rubber fumes in Akron, where some of the richest tournaments have been held, choke me. I am allergic to foam rubber and many other elements.

In 1969, I determined to throw off my inhibitions and compete in a couple of tournaments in Florida. In the National Airlines tournament at Miami, I broke out in a rash, my eyes became blood-shot and I could hardly move my legs. I had to withdraw and spend two weeks on my back.

I felt sufficiently recovered to play in the Masters, a tournament I have never won, and, surprising to me, I led through the first three rounds. Leading by a shot going into the final round and playing the best golf of my career at Augusta, I felt confident that finally I might qualify for one of those coveted green coats.

On the final day, my game collapsed. I couldn't explain it. Shirley, my wife, followed me around the course. She said she had never seen me play worse. I was flat. My touch was gone. I had no control over my shots.

This was one of the great disappointments of my life, but I refused to become discouraged. I took the optimistic view. I felt that it was remarkable that I could play as well as I did through the first three rounds after being ill for two weeks. On the last day, I simply ran out of gas. I had nothing left.

Thus golf, like life, is a succession of hills and valleys, happiness and heartaches, delirium and disappointment. The errors and poor shots I have made—and they have been plenty—are constructive aids toward improvement. The mistakes serve as fruitful material for shaping a better next. Each experience on the golf course, as in life, has been a source of enrichment.

If I could pass one bit of advice on to

readers of this book, it would be this: Let golf be a miniature replica of your life. Learn and work hard. Think positively. Accept the challenge. Don't let frustrations throw you. Keep cool, swing easy, play within yourself and have fun. Above all, have fun.

It's All One Game

When golfers gather in the locker rooms, they frequently argue over the relative importance of the various clubs. Which phase is better to master—the long game or the short game? If there was a choice, would you prefer to be a good driver or a good putter? Which more vitally affects the putting?

I have heard some golfers say that golf is divided into two different games. One is the game of moving the ball from the tee to the green. This is a game played solely in the air. The other is the game of getting the ball into the hole—chipping and putting. It is played on the ground.

I strongly disagree with this premise. It is all one game. The strokes are all the same, played with a varying degree of force. The grip, the rhythm, the body movement from left to right do not change. What does change is the violence of the stroke and its subtlety as the ball gets closer to the cup.

The drive is very important. Normally it accounts for 50 percent of the distance. It gets the ball in play. Executed properly, it sets up the ball for the shot to the green. A good drive can set the pattern for the round, buoy confidence and make scoring easier. It is true that half the strokes of most rounds are spent around the green. It is also obvious that the quicker you get there—and in the calmest frame of mind— the more satisfactory will be the final result.

This brings us to a point I made earlier. That is that placement is more important than power off the tee. So the first advice I would give anyone standing on a tee and looking down the green corridor that forms the fairway is this: Don't try to be a hero. Don't try to murder the ball. Just manage it. This is best done by knowing what constitutes a sound swing—this comes from homework—and then executing it as smoothly and effectively as possible.

First of all, you must eliminate fear. For some reason—quite understandably, I might say—knees start knocking, nerves tighten up and the head starts reeling once a man tees up the ball and reaches for the biggest and most awesome weapon in his bag. I say this sudden stage fright is understandable, but it isn't necessary, and it only tends to make the golfer blow the shot.

Don't Press

During my caddying days back in San Diego, I regularly carried a bag for a prominent doctor who had a great passion for golf. He loved the game, worked hard at it and seemed to relish the week-ends on which he was free to play.

I recall one incident that has stayed with me as a vivid reminder.

Playing the first hole on this particular course—not a tremendously long but at the same time not an easy hole—my employer caught hold of an excellent drive. He reached the green with a nice nine-iron.

On the second day, he hit another good drive on the same hole. As he had done previously, he pulled a nine-iron and again put the ball on the green.

Then came the third day. This time, the doctor was not so fortunate. He sliced the ball into the rough and, although he had a satisfactory lie, he was a good 120 yards for the green.

"The nine-iron," the doctor said to me.

"But, Sir," I protested, "it is more than a nine-iron. I suggest you take a seven or at least an eight."

"The nine!" the doctor insisted with irritation.

I gave into his request. He took the nine-iron, whaled into the ball with all his strength, and left the ball short and wide of the mark.

I didn't rub it in.

"I know," the doctor said, apologetically. "I knew I probably should have hit a bigger club, but I wanted to see if I couldn't reach the green three times in a row with a nine-iron."

The episode accented one of the most common errors in golf—that of over-reaching. It is a common frailty. Sometimes we try to accomplish too much with too little. We use bad judgment. We try to be a hero. We turn an easy assignment into a hard one.

It is a point we discussed earlier in the book. That is the advisability in golf not to press, not to try to overpower a shot but always to play well within one's self. If this be sound advice in the case of a tee shot, it is doubly sound in the matter of the irons.

The irons offer the gateway to good scoring. Certainly, it is a thrill to hear the head of a driver clack against the ball and then to watch the ball sail to a good position on the fairway. There is an equal thrill in watching the ball describe a perfect parabola and then settle down gently onto a spacious green.

Every golfer, whether he be a hardened tournament pro or a week-end buff, heaves a sigh of relief when he finally plants the ball on the putting surface. There's not one of us at that precise moment who doesn't nurture the hope of getting down in one— wherever the ball is from the pin.

Frequently a player doesn't give himself this fighting chance because his eyes are bigger than that little mechanism in the top of his head which is calling signals. He refuses to take into account his own restrictions. He tries to emulate the pros. He goes for broke. And, much to his own distress, he usually blows the shot.

The Club's the Thing

I remember a few years ago, there was a golfer on the tour rated by his contemporaries as one of the finest shotmakers the game had ever produced. He lived up to this reputation by winning his share of tournaments, including the major ones. But, as his career progressed, he became increasingly nervous on the course. He also became painstakingly slow, often standing over a shot for seeming minutes before striking the ball. He studied the terrain, sometimes changed his mind several times before selecting the club he used. His game deteriorated well before its time and he dropped completely from competition.

Around locker rooms, his fellow golfers debated theories on why so marvelous a talent should reach the end of the road so soon. Then one of the player's closest friends came up with this unique explanation:

"If he would let me club him around a

golf course, I guarantee he would never lose a tournament. He is such a gifted shotmaker—he can do so much with so many different clubs—that his brilliance has turned his own worst enemy.

"When he walks up to a shot he automatically starts wondering, 'Should I hit a strong eight or an easy seven?' 'Should I chip and run this seven or punch a wedge at the stick?' 'Is this a three-wood or a two-iron?' He could hit any shot in the bag and do a lot with any one club, but his versatility was such that he became a nervous wreck. He got to a point where he couldn't hit any club well."

This is unlikely to happen to the average golfer but there is a deep-seated lesson in the case. While golf definitely is a thinking man's game, there is danger in trying to think too much. There is only one brain and a thousand muscles. It is possible—as in this instance—to outsmart yourself.

It is best to know exactly what you can do with a certain club. When a situation arises calling for that club, don't second guess. Walk up to the shot and execute it. You'll be surprised—if you've grounded yourself thoroughly in fundamentals—how well the shot will come off. You must still rely on instinct.

Naturally, a golfer may adopt certain clubs as his favorites. He gets a better feel with them. He has more confidence when he wraps his fingers around the shaft. For instance, a player may feel that he can hit a seven-iron better than any club in his bag. A situation may come which may require a six-iron. The player goes to "Old Reliable" No. 7. He fails to reach the green. On a longer shot, he may choose a three-iron over a No. 2 because he feels he is steadier with it. So he risks some length for safety.

I am a firm believer in percentages. But I feel that golfers who take this attitude are similar to cripples who are content always to get around on a crutch.

There are 14 clubs in the bag—I use the pro quota simply to get my point across. The good golfer should learn to master every one. The way to do it is to use them all.

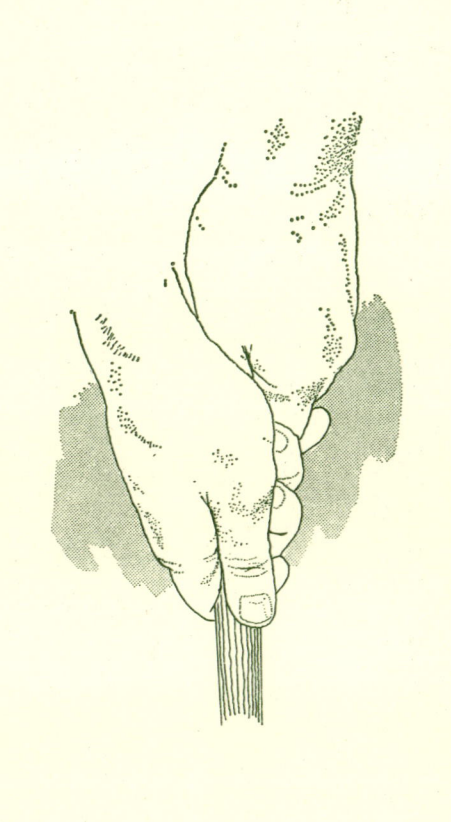

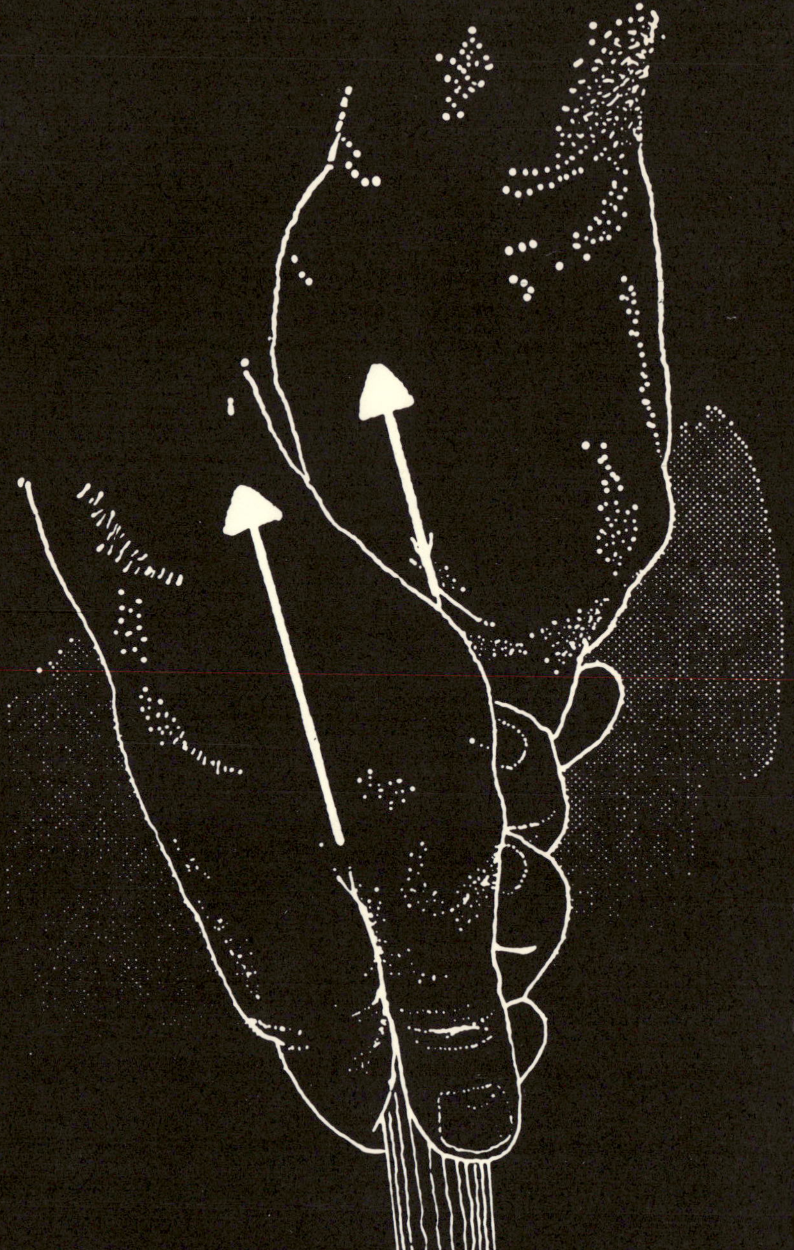

The Grip

The grip is the most important fundamental in golf, and perhaps the most neglected. Only about one in a hundred golfers uses a proper grip. Yet it is the player's only contact with the ball. The hands make contact with the club and the club head with the ball. The power that is built up in the body—first from the legs, up through the hips and then through the shoulders and arms—is transmitted to the club through the hands.

The grip thus becomes the outlet—the gear box—for all of the body's generated power. If it is faulty, the entire swing can go to pieces. Most teachers contend that good golf begins with a good grip. A bad grip is certain to result in years of wasted power, scattershot golf and frustration.

Whereas swings may differ with the individual golfer, the grip is standard. It has been for half a century. In that period, the world has changed drastically. Man has mechanized the world, conquered space and in golf made vast improvements in equipment and techniques, yet no one has been able to improve on the grip introduced by an English stylist named Harry Vardon before the turn of the century.

It is still referred to as the Vardon overlapping grip. There are mild variations—the interlocking grip and the so-called baseball grip in which the hands do not overlap at all—but they follow Vardon's basic principle of finger pressure. And the Vardon grip is used by perhaps ninety per cent of the topflight players.

Vardon won six British Open Championships between 1896 and 1914 and became a model for style and skill on the Isle where the game was supposedly born.

As a youngster in his native Jersey, Vardon joined his companions in playing golf in an abandoned field with marble taws and clubs hewn from oak tree branches. The shafts were so rough that they produced calluses on the palms of the hands. Vardon, to escape these blisters, developed the light, finger grip. Thus the Vardon grip was born.

To achieve the proper grip, the hands must be cemented together. They must work as a unit, like a hinge. The best way would be to hold the palms of the hands together as in an applauding position. However, this isn't practical because it is impossible to hold the club that way. So the hands are joined in another fashion.

To achieve this grip, you start with the

left hand. It does the work. Place the club in the left hand diagonally across the palm so that the shaft is pressed under the pad at the inside heel of the palm and lies directly across the top joint of the forefinger. The last three fingers close snugly over the shaft. The forefinger crooks around the shaft and the thumb falls into a natural position. The forefinger and thumb play a secondary role, providing steadiness and feel.

The two middle fingers provide the pressure for the right hand, which is the overlapping hand. Place the club in the right hand so that the shaft lies across the top joint of the four fingers and below the palm. Fold the right hand over the left thumb, letting the right thumb run down the left side of the shaft. The little finger of the right hand overlaps the index finger of the left hand, forming a link.

Vardon always disliked the term "grip," contending it did not connote properly the relations of the hands with the shaft. He considered it more of a gentle "hold" or almost a "caress." It is imperative that the club be held in the fingers and not in the palm of the hand. Also the player must reject the tendency to permit the right forefinger and the thumb to take charge. This causes one to lurch into the ball.

Once the grip is fixed, it may be checked with visual guidelines handed down by teachers through the years. Most pros advise that when you look down at your hands at the address of the ball you see the first two knuckles of the left hand and the "Vs" of both hands—angles formed by your thumbs and forefingers gripping the club—pointing toward your right shoulder. This varies according to the individual. Hogan prefers that the "V" point to the button of the chin.

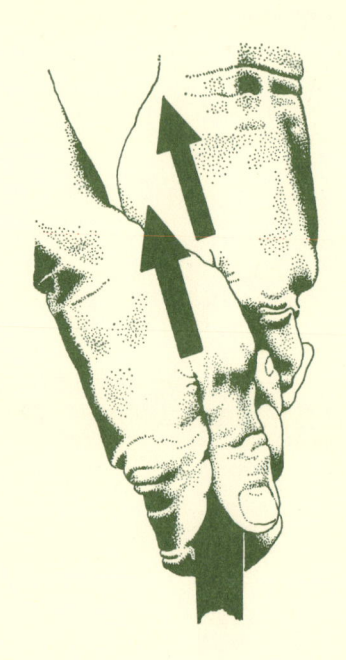

On the interlocking grip, the little finger of the right hand, instead of overlapping the left index finger, is stuck between the first two fingers of the left hand. The left index finger goes between the last two fingers of the right hand. This grip has been found more practical for players with small hands, including Gene Sarazen, Lloyd Mangrum and Jack Nicklaus.

Bob Rosburg became the most prominent exponent of the baseball grip. The two hands are placed on the shaft independently, next to each other. Like the Vardon grip, it is a finger grip with the main pressure applied by the last three fingers of the left hand and middle two fingers of the right.

The prescribed grip may seem awkward at first. It isn't the way you would normally hold a broom or pick up a suitcase. As mentioned before, the natural tendency is to work with the right hand. In golf, the work load is carried by the left side of the body, hands included.

I have gone into considerable detail on the grip because I feel that is basic to good golf. Also it is more standardized—less subject to individual physiques and whims—than the other phases of the game. The matters of stance and swing will be explored on the ensuing pages in which we take up situations shot by shot.

The Grip

Deciding just how to take the grip is sometimes confusing to the average golfer. There is, however, a definite relationship between the grip and the clubface that, if adopted, can be very helpful.

If you are unsure about your grip, make it a point to align the palm of your left hand with the clubface (see illustration). The latter, of course, should face the target or, to put it another way, be perpendicular to the intended line of flight.

When this is done, you will have the best chance of achieving a solid hit, with the face on line with the target. All you have to do is make sure the back of your left hand swings toward the target at and after impact for as long as possible.

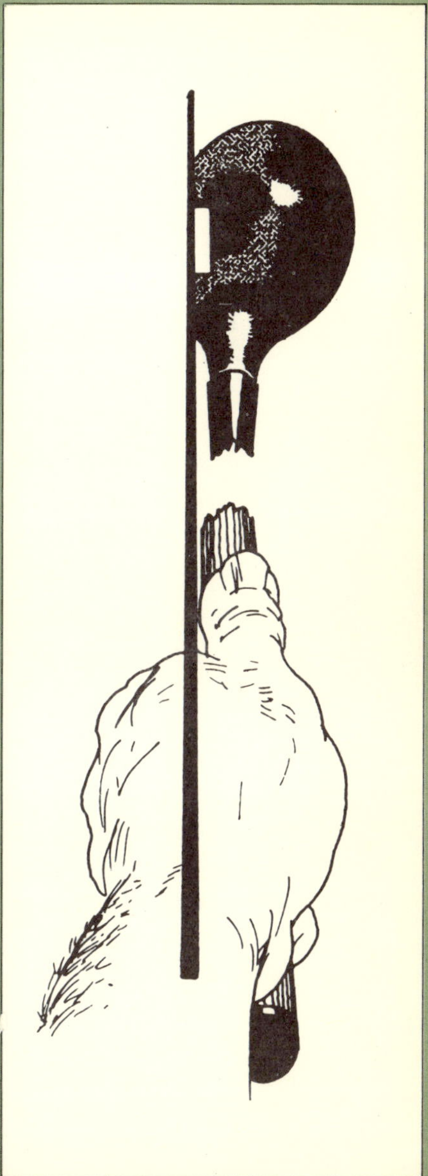

To play your best, take a grip which allows your wrists to hinge naturally as you swing. The best grip is more in the fingers than the palms.

The left hand controls positioning and is placed on the club first. As illustrated, the butt end is placed in the crease of the palm below the little finger. The club then runs diagonally across the middle of the forefinger. When the hand is folded over the club, the thumb should be slightly right of center, with the last three fingers gripping firmly. The "V" formed by the thumb and forefinger should point approximately to the right shoulder.

Extreme variations from this will inhibit the wrist hinge.

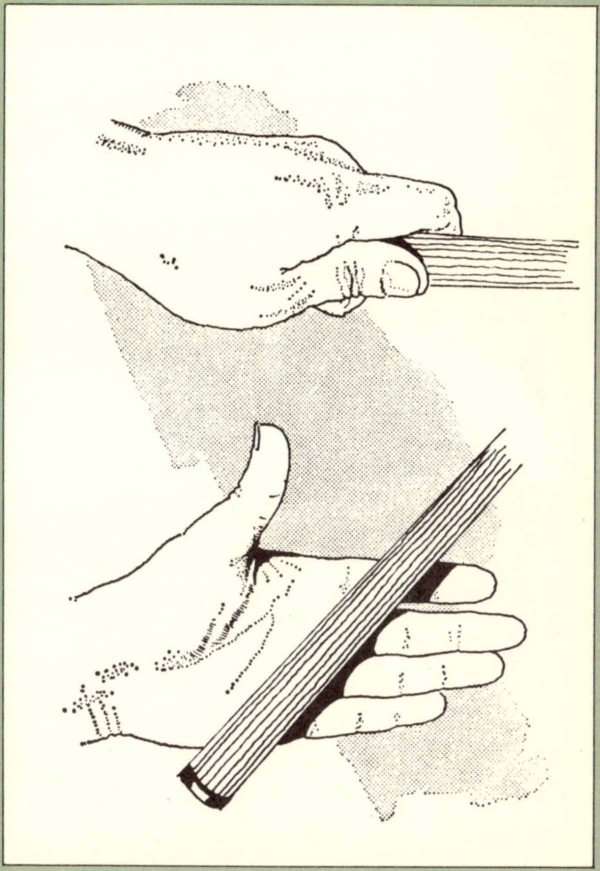

The right-hand grip should be in the fingers for most effective feel and sensitivity. A palm grip produces a ham-handed sensation not conducive to a "lively" swing.

When the right hand is opened, you should see the club run from the junction of the little finger across the middle of the forefinger. In the popular Vardon overlap grip, the right little finger curls over the left forefinger. Fold your right hand over the club so that the "V" formed by the thumb and forefinger points in the same direction as the lefthand "V." This places the right thumb slightly to left of center on top of the club.

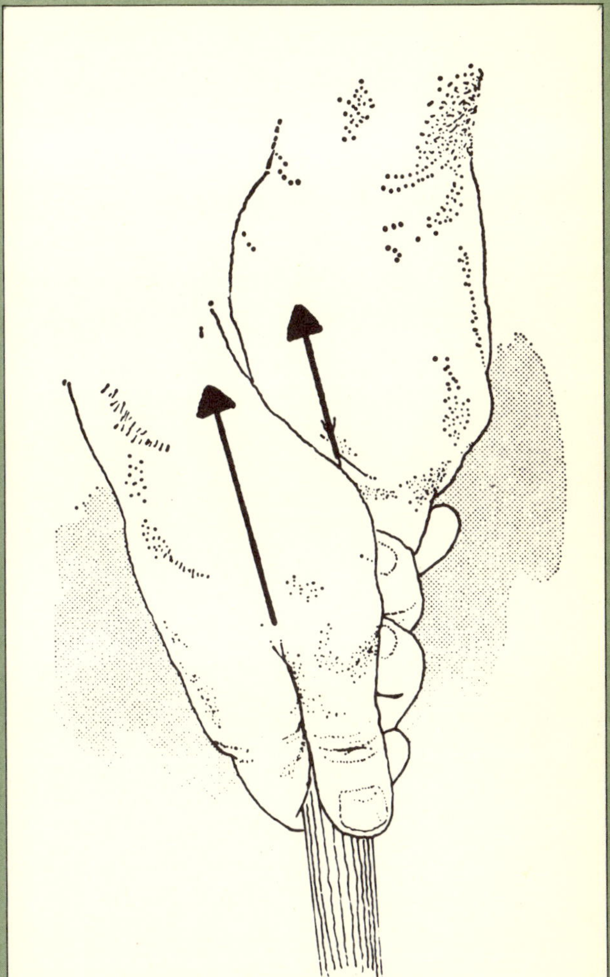

While your grip on the club should never be intense, there are some pressure points all golfers should know.

Since the left hand is placed on the club first, let's talk about it. The most pressure should be felt in the last three fingers (see shaded area in the illustration). This firmness should be especially felt at the top of the backswing, for if they loosen at this point, control will be lost.

In the right hand, firmness should be felt in the thumb and forefinger, not so much at address and during the backswing, but at impact Should they loosen there, the clubface may move "out of square" and an off-line shot may result.

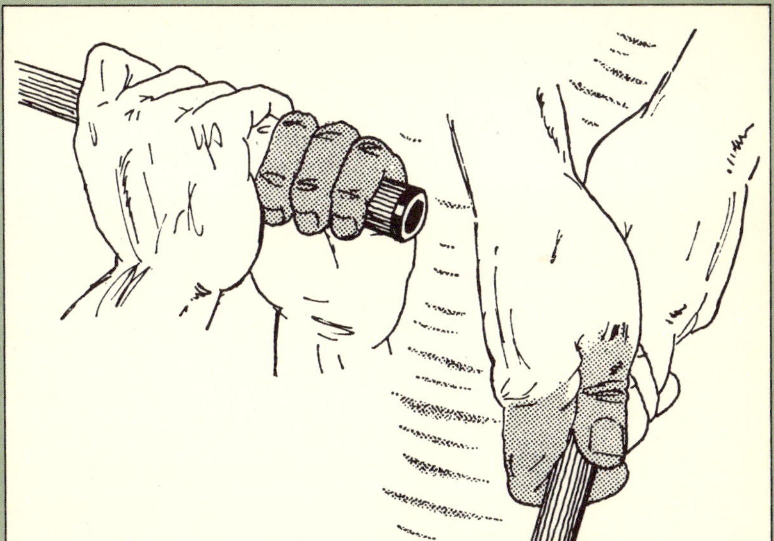

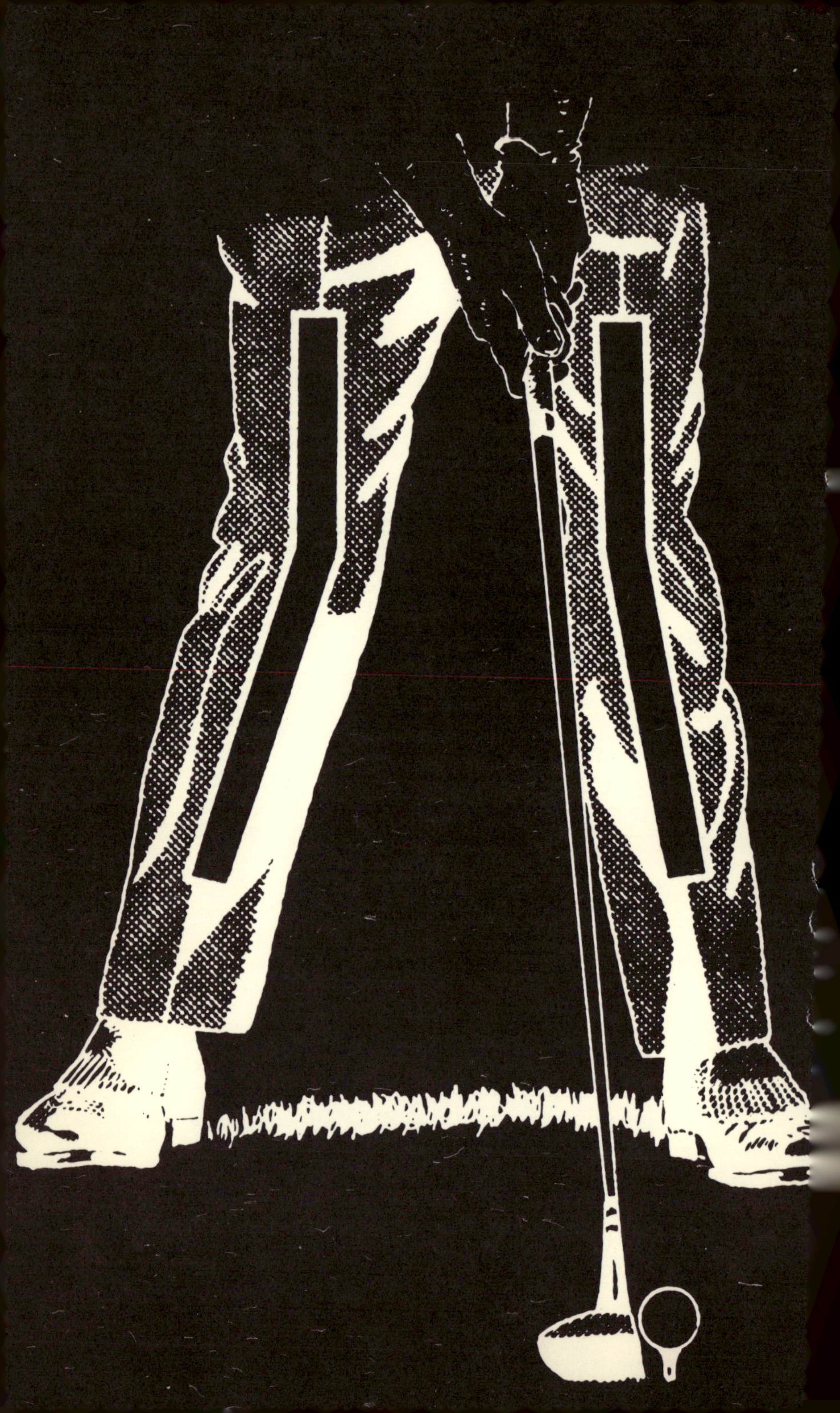

The Stance

The stance is largely standard with most top golfers. The right foot is at a right angle to the line of flight. The left foot is pointed slightly to the left. Some tournament golfers like to have the toes of both feet pointed out. I do not hold that foot position must be basic. The main thing is to be comfortable.

The stance provides balance. It determines direction. The player learns the foot placement that is less awkward and more effective for him through trial and error. Once he has established a stance to his liking, he should try to make it instinctive and second nature.

There are basic rules on the width of the stance. It normally varies with the type of club being used. The stance is wider in playing woods and long irons. The feet are closer together in using lofted clubs. On medium irons, my practice is to place my feet apart about the width of my shoulders. A tendency to be avoided is that of taking too wide a stance in using the driver. This can prevent fluid hip action. But remember: The key is comfort.

The Stance

There are three basic stances in golf, and each produces a different result.

For most players, the square stance is best on all full shots with longer clubs. In this stance, the feet are equidistant from the intended line of flight. This encourages a clubhead path on line to the target which will most likely produce a straight shot.

The open stance has the left foot withdrawn more from the intended line than the right. At best, this tends to produce a slight fade from left to right. Overdone, it will cause a slice.

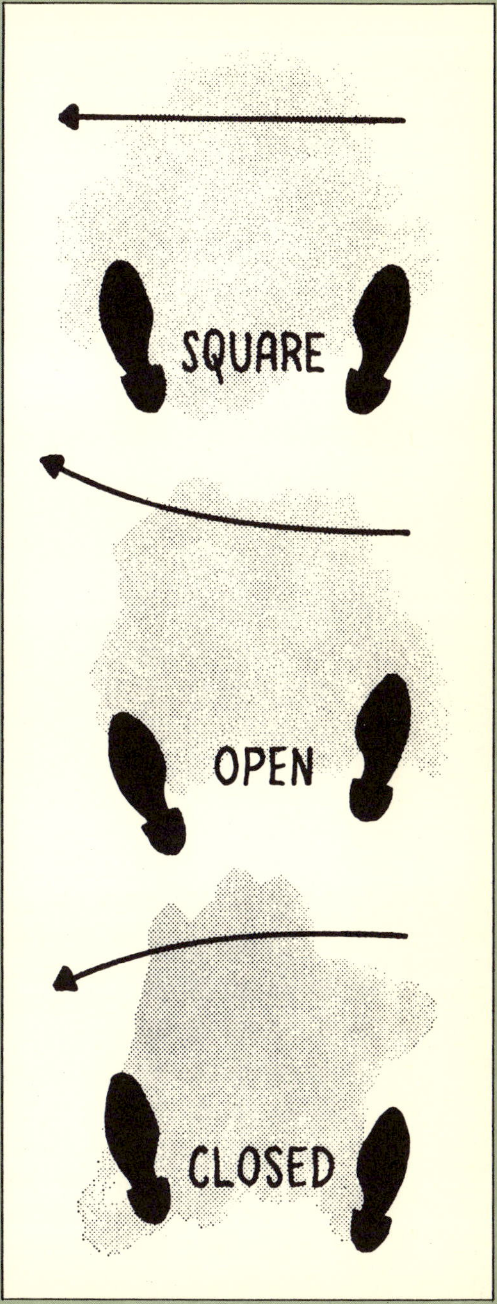
SQUARE
OPEN
CLOSED

Those who establish a certain pattern in taking the stance will find it easier to take a proper address position every time.

When you've decided on the stance you wish to take, stand directly opposite the ball with both feet close together. The ball should be more or less on a line between your feet. Now, move your left foot toward the target to its prescribed position. Take a check to see that the ball is aligned the way you want it aligned, off your left heel. Finally, move your right foot into its position.

The illustration shows the stance for the drive.

ONE

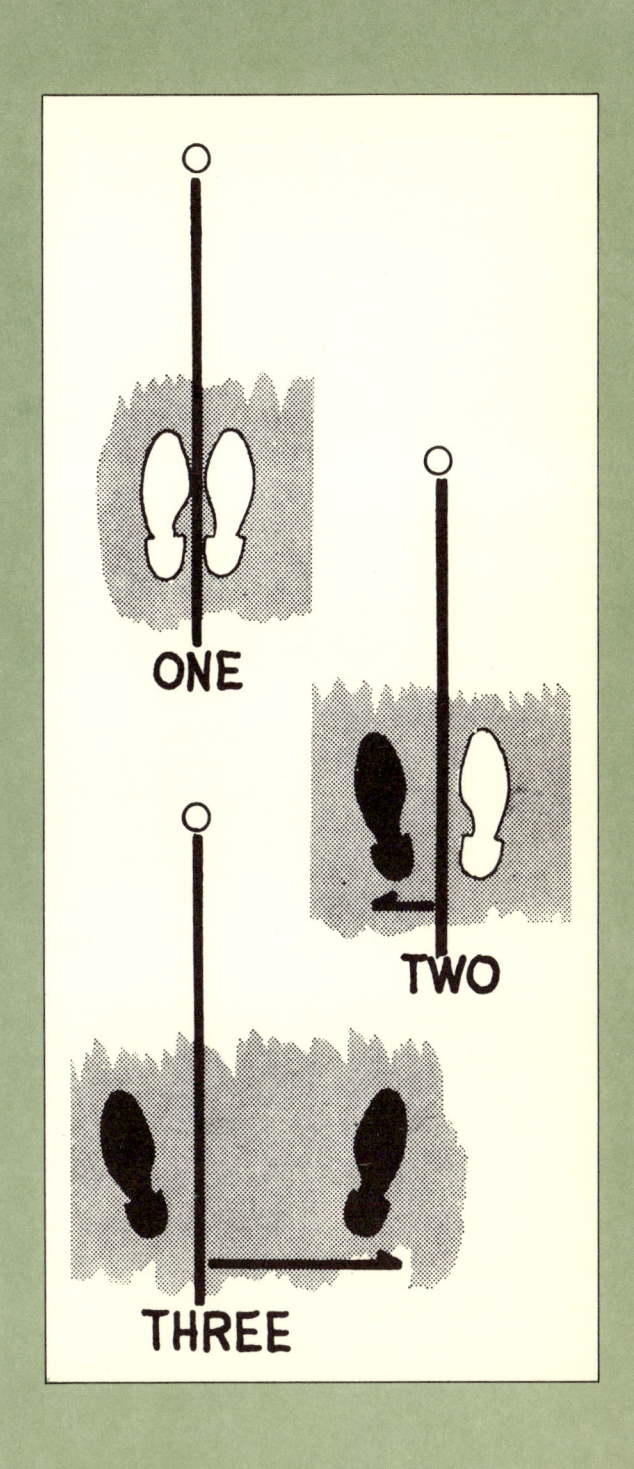

TWO

THREE

Correct stance on full shots finds left toe turned out about 45 degrees and the right foot almost perpendicular to the line of flight. Positioned this way, you're less likely to sway away from the target on the backswing. The right foot acts as a preventive brace.

When the left foot is turned out, a path is prepared for the down-and-through part of the swing. The left hip must be cleared, or pivoted, out of the way during the downswing. If it is not, the hands will be impeded and a weaker shot, probably off to the right, will result.

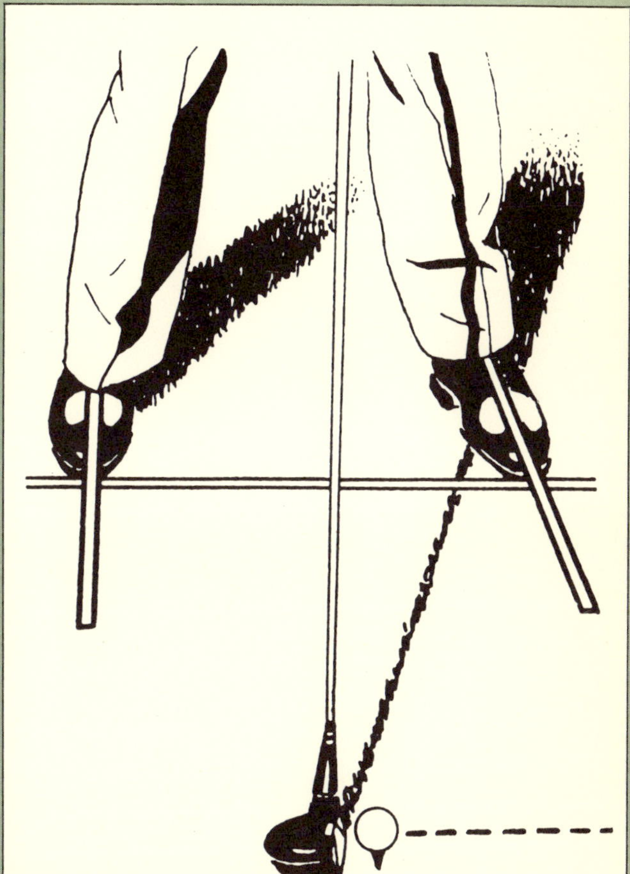

In a way, golf is a knock-kneed game. It is infinitely better to keep your weight inside your body at all times, rather than letting it drift outside. If you allow the latter to happen, you will probably sway off the target or lose your balance, or both.

Start out at address with both knees flexed slightly inward. At this point, the right knee should be "in" a little more than the left, as illustrated. The inward right knee will help prevent a sway away from the target on the backswing. The inward left knee helps keep the weight from moving to the outside of the left foot during the downswing and impact moves.

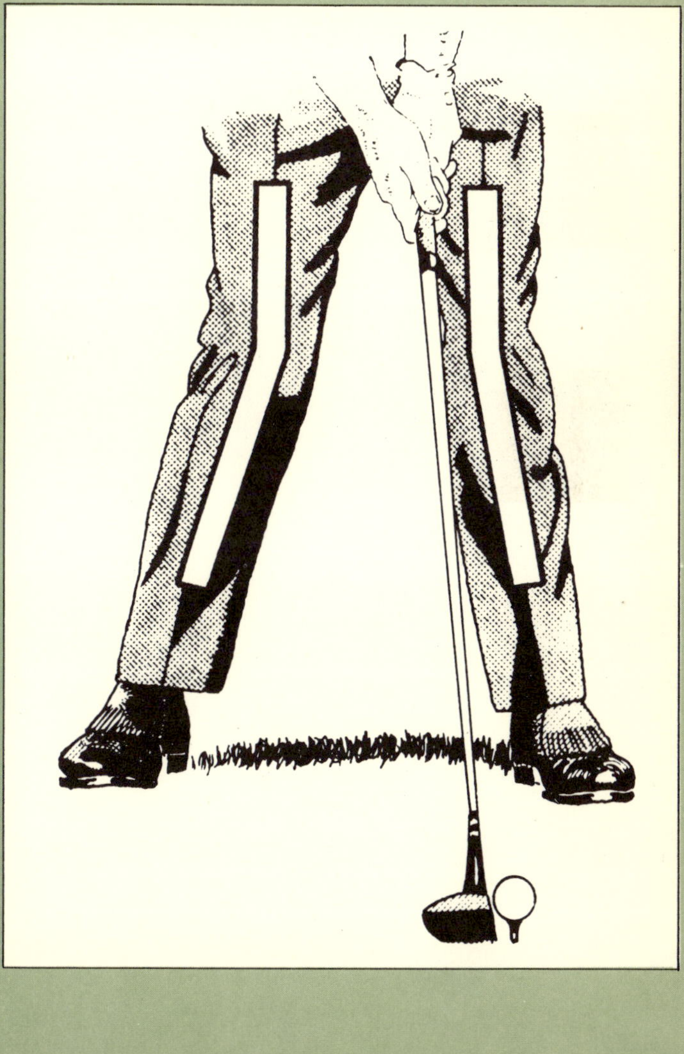

For drives, tee the ball so that half of it appears above the top of the clubhead when the latter is at rest in the address position.

You are then able to impact the ball at the clubface center when the clubhead is properly just past the lowest point of its downswing arc. This will naturally lift the ball into a correct trajectory for distance and accuracy.

If you tee the ball lower, you might bear down on it, making your downswing too steep, causing a hook or slice. Teed higher, the clubhead may sweep under the ball and pop it up high into the air. This will cut distance.

TEEING TIPS

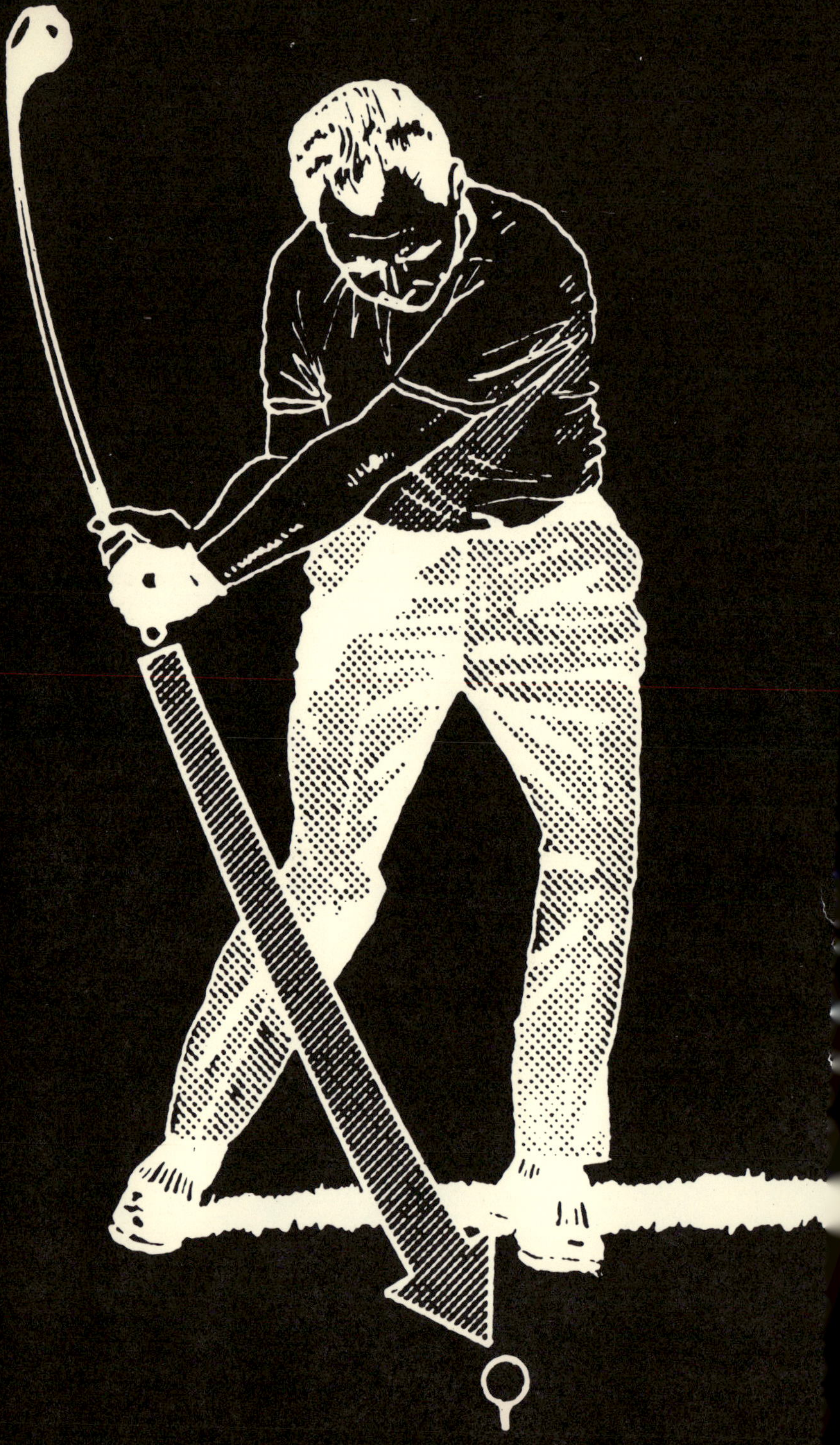

The Swing

As we have mentioned previously, swings differ according to the individual. All have one thing in common. To be effective, they must be compact. All moving parts work together. They should be as solid and as dependable as a metal hinge.

On the full swing, the clubhead is brought back until the shaft behind the back is horizontal to the ground. For some, it is so exaggerated that the club dips toward the earth. On the three-quarter swing, the shaft is at about a 45 degree angle while on the short, or half, swing the club, in reaching its zenith, is pointing virtually straight into the air.

The fullness of the swing doesn't necessarily affect the distance of the shot. The point to remember—no matter which of the swings you use—is to take care that the swing does not get away from you. This can happen by breaking the wrists or loosening the grip in the club. If the fundamentals of the grip, stance and swing are followed, the shot will come off properly whether you use a wide, flowing arc or, as in the case of Doug Sanders, swing as if you were in a telephone booth.

You also hear discussions of the upright and flat swings. Which is the more effective? Which is preferred? This, too, is largely a matter of the individual and the golfer's taste. On the upright swing, the club is brought straight up, with the clubhead pointing into the sky at its apex, and then brought down sharply on the downswing. The flat swing is more horizontal, more similar to the swing of a baseball bat at a low-pitched ball.

Jack Nicklaus has a pronounced upright swing. Arnold Palmer's swing would be described as flat, although it is not as extreme as that of some other top golfers. My own swing is more on the upright side. I have sought to try to keep it from being too exaggerated either way.

The Driver

The design of the driver—or any wood club for that matter—tends to create a feeling of uneasiness. Built for distance, it has the longest shaft. It has a face which is almost flat. The bottom of the head, or sole, is also flat. Because the ball is swept off the tee or grass and the club does not bite into the turf, as in the case of irons, there is less natural feel and less confidence.

The driver is the hardest of all clubs to master. It requires the greatest precision and control. No other club—unless perhaps it be the putter—causes the top professionals greater concern. Most of them are constantly fighting it.

The secret of a good drive is restraint. Once the grip and fundamentals of the swing are mastered, the crux then lies in smooth and effortless execution. The smoother and more relaxed the better. Never consciously try for distance. Distance will come naturally if the timing is good.

It must be natural. Any attempt to pour more power into the swing through sheer ferocity or lunging at the ball can throw the whole procedure out of kilter. Instead of a booming drive, you wind up normally with a mess of misery.

The backswing is the key. Bring the club back smoothly and slowly without breaking your wrists. The left hand, left arm and left knee all work together in a single, well-coordinated pattern. Once the clubhead is brought back as far as it can go, there should be a slight pause—only the slightest—and then the recoil action.

Just as in the backswing the hands initiate the action and the order moves to the arms, shoulders and hips, on the downswing the flow of the action is reversed. The hips start the downswing and become the pivotal point of the continuous action. Then shoulders, arms and hands unleash like a giant spring.

I have always felt that some teachers put too much stress on the shifting of the weight. I think the weight shifts naturally. As the club is brought back, the natural tendency of the body action will be to throw the weight to the right foot. As the clubhead is brought down, the weight automatically shifts to the left foot.

How many things can a golfer think about as he is preparing to hit the ball, anyway? In attempting to remember all the advice—head steady, left arm straight, wrists unbroken, remember to pivot, shift the weight, back slowly now, pause at the top, start down with the hips—a golfer can become so confused that he is apt to hit the ball to the rear or miss it completely. Both have been done.

For myself, I sometimes must check myself on the backswing. I become overly anxious and swing too quickly. Generally, the thing I think about on the tee is where I want to hit the ball—what position I would like to be in for my second shot. Other points should come instinctively and the mind should be clear once you are ready to drive the ball.

For the average golfer, however, it is wise to remember two factors before hitting a drive—keep the head still and keep the wrists stiff. The shift of body weight, the coordination of hands, arms, shoulders and hips will take care of themselves.

The Swing

In the address position, the back of the left hand faces the target and moves directly at the target at and after impact.

This assures accuracy, since the left hand controls the direction the clubface moves. My hands are working well together when I can achieve this left hand position. After impact, I swing the back of the left hand on out toward the target for as long as possible. Of course, the hit is a two-handed affair, with the right tossing in its power.

The closed stance finds the right foot farther from the intended line than the left. This will produce a draw from right to left, or, if overdone, a hook well to the left.

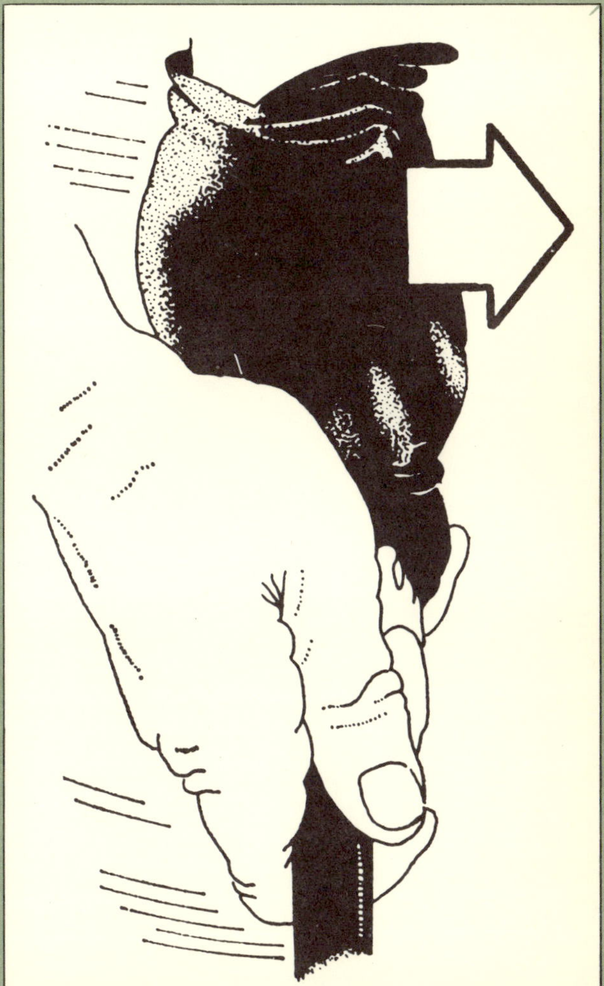

The position of the right elbow at address does affect the backswing arc. The inside of the right elbow should face away from the golfer or at about a 9-degree angle from the target. The right arm should be especially free of tension, with the elbow bent and its tip almost touching the golfer's body (see illustration). Positioned this way, the right arm will bend or "fold" easily during the backswing and the right elbow will stay comfortably close to the body. Slicing is thus minimized.

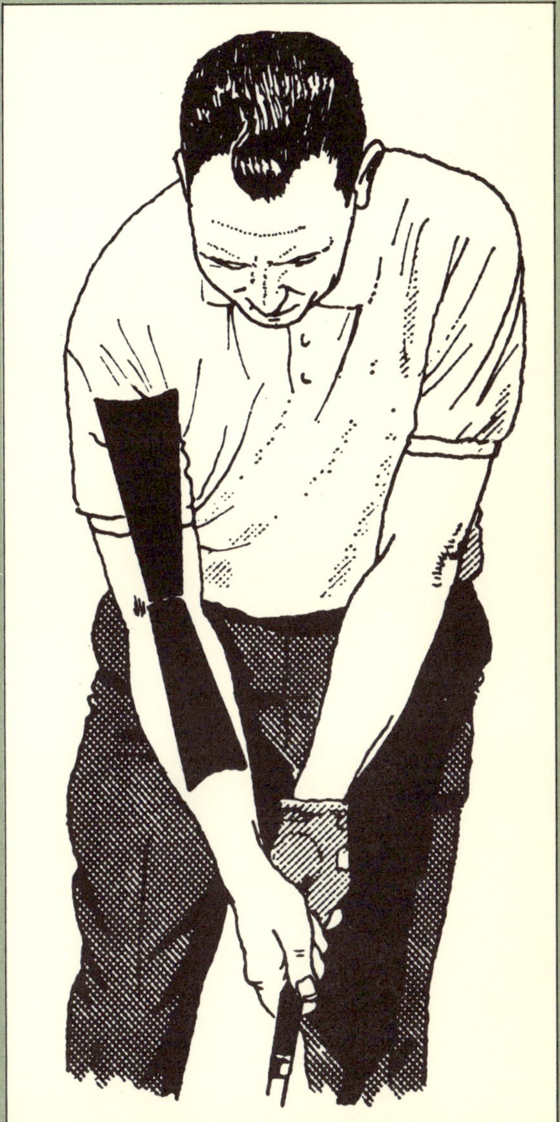

For most golfers, the left hand should be about a hand's breadth from the left leg at address for the driver. That is, the "little finger" side of the hand should be about six inches from the body at this point (see illustration). For shots with shorter clubs, this distance, of course, decreases.

The only way to check this is to have a friend take a look at your address position. If the left hand is farther away, you may tip forward toward your toes later on in the swing. If it's closer, you'll probably rock back on your heels at impact.

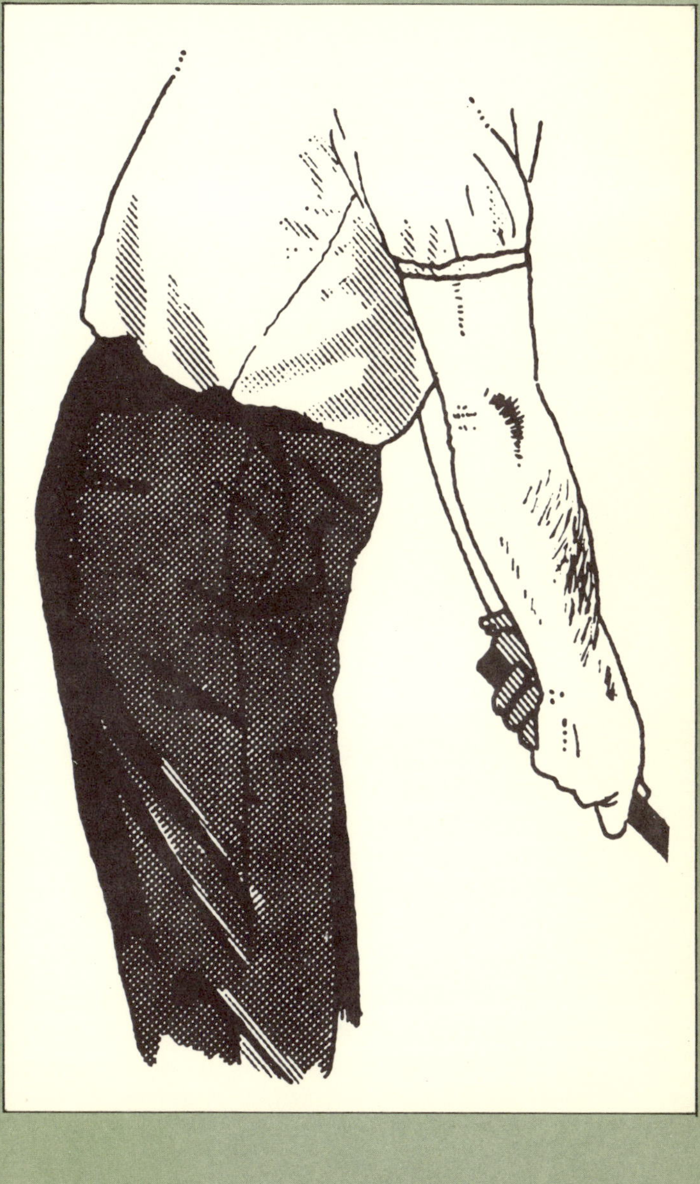

If the wind is behind you, play the ball about an inch farther forward than usual off the left toe instead of the left instep, if the latter's your usual position. The ball can be teed up a quarter-inch or so higher.

Hit the ball a little past the bottom of your swing arc (see illustration).

At address, your hands may be an inch or so behind the ball. Use your normal stance, but aim a little to the left because such shots tend to fade to the right. Now take your biggest swing and finish very high and upright.

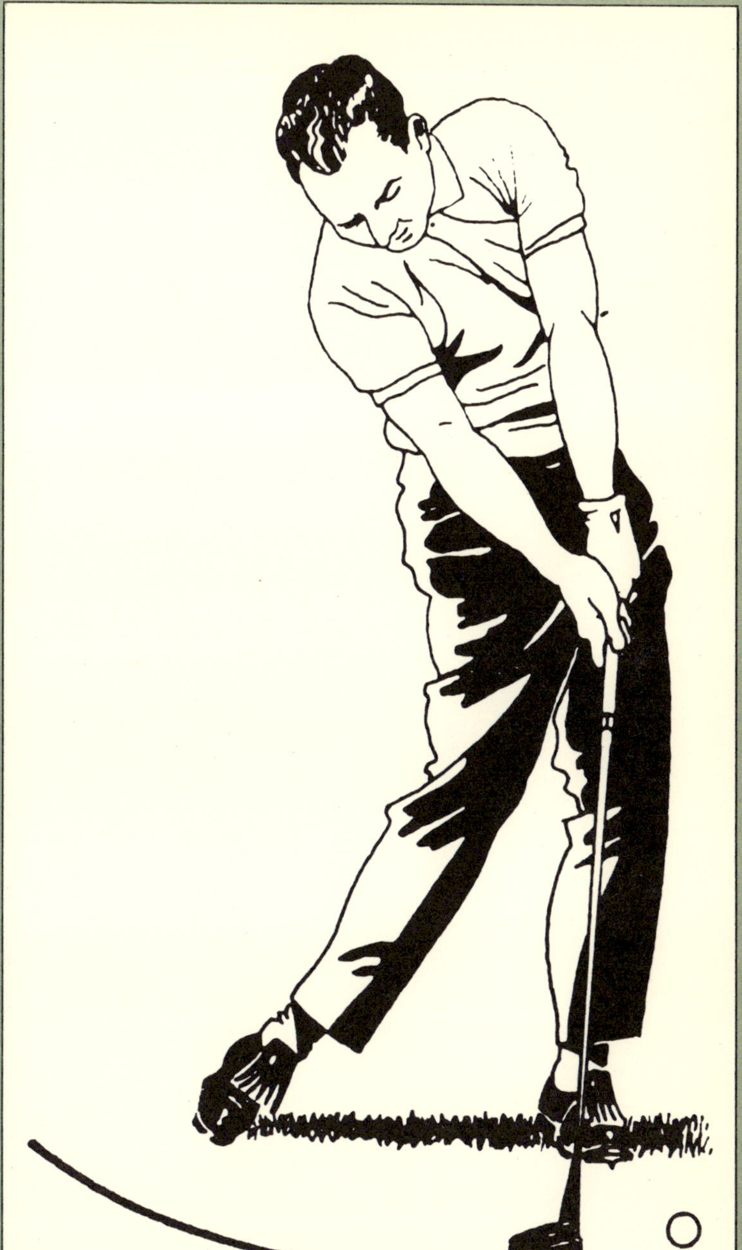

Waggling the clubhead over the ball before bringing the club back will get you used to the motion of the swing. It is not a good idea to try to start the swing from a dead start, which is what would be happening if the waggle were eliminated.

Cultivate a smooth, swinging waggle until you use the procedure before every swing. Move the clubhead back and then over the ball before you place it in position to start the backswing. This way your hands and fingers get used to the idea of holding the club while it is in motion.

I use only two waggles, then get the swing in motion without too much delay. You may need more waggles, but stick to the same procedure every time for consistency.

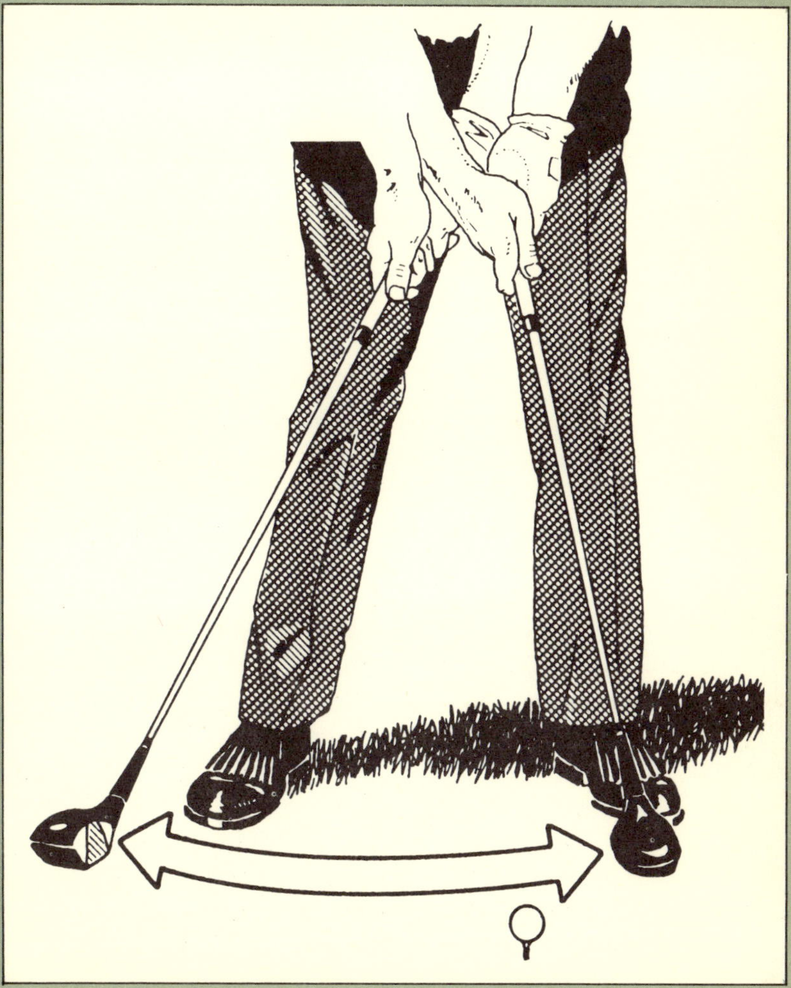

Imagination has much to do with the golf swing. Imagining how the clubhead should impact the ball will actually lead to a subconscious movement of your body muscles to that end.

The best clubhead path in the impact area is from inside to inside. That is, the clubhead swings into the ball from slightly inside the intended line, touches that line momentarily as the clubface contacts the ball, then moves back inside the line as the follow-through develops (see illustration).

This will produce the most solid and square impact and send the ball along a straight line. Before you swing, keep this swing arc in mind . . . and you may be surprised to see how often you can achieve it.

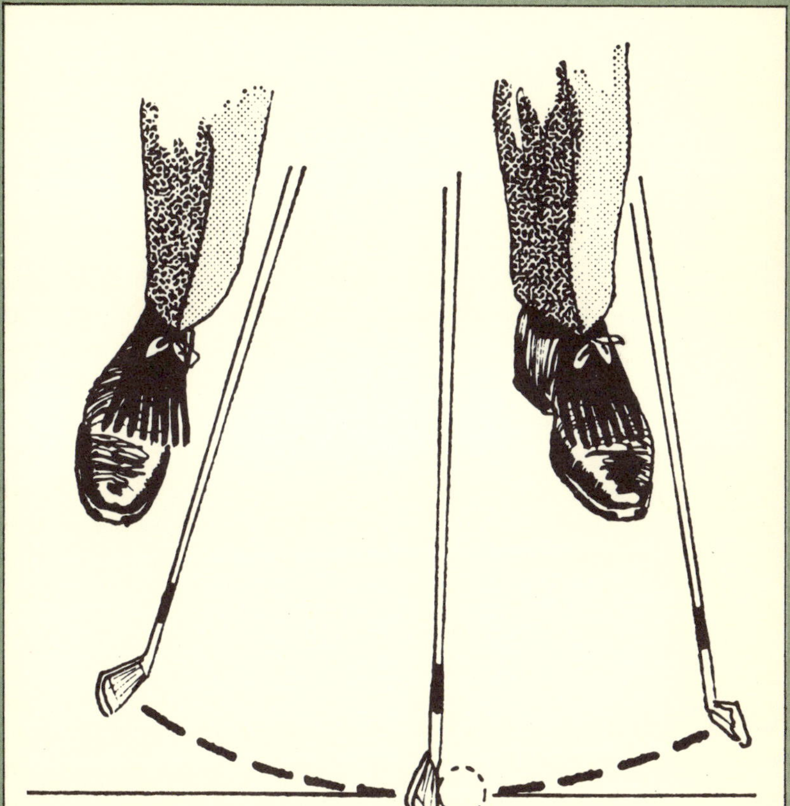

One of the greatest distance-killing errors in the golf swing is the sway away from the target on the backswing. When this happens, the swing as a whole is robbed of the necessary centrifugal action which eventually results in good distance.

If you are not getting the distance you think you should, check possible movement of your right leg during the backswing. It should remain in the same relative position at the top as it was at address. A good way to check this in practice is to place a stick in the ground just outside your right foot. If your knee hits it when you swing, you're swaying. Continue practicing until your right leg remains in place during the backswing.

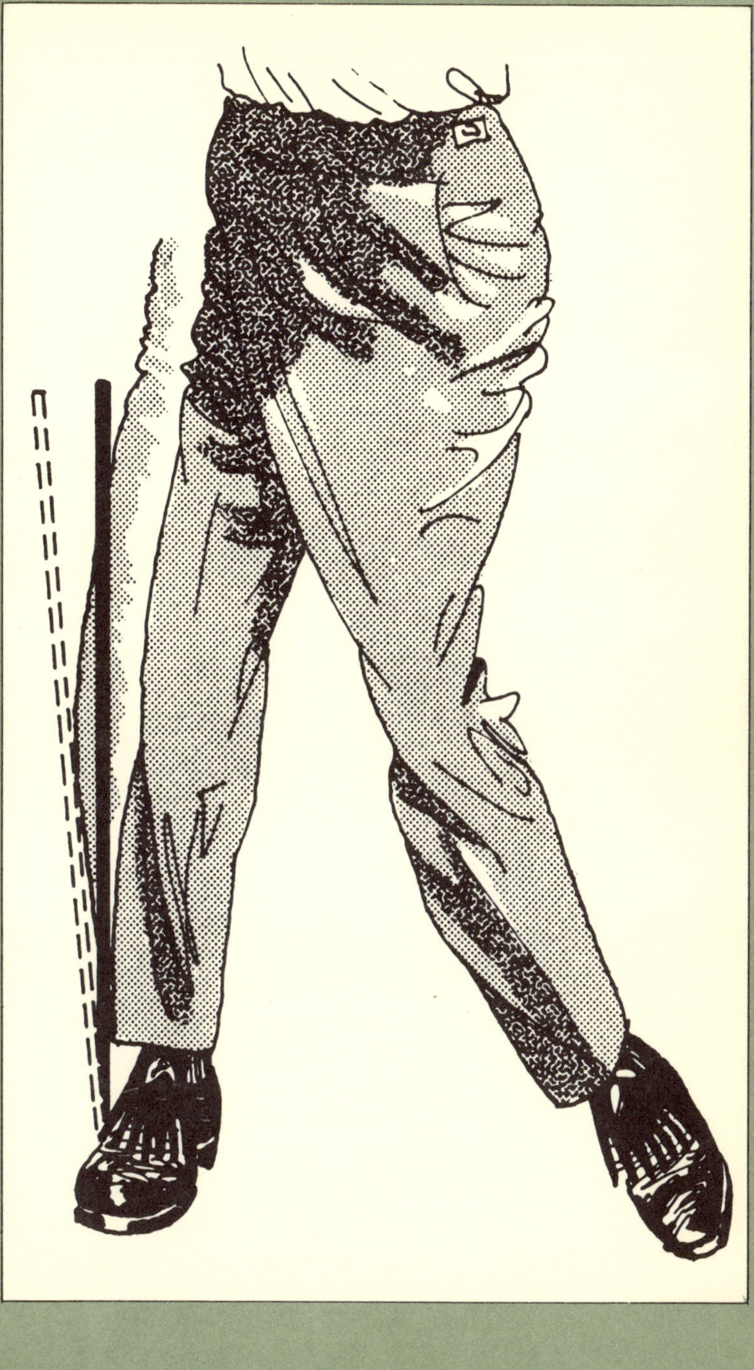

The Backswing

As the backswing begins, with the left hand, arm and shoulder in control, the wrists remain as they were at address—straight—until later on when they begin to cock about halfway up. This passive beginning (illustrated) serves to keep the clubface square to the intended line at this most important part of the swing. Much of the "battle" for a good swing is won if the motion is started in this manner.

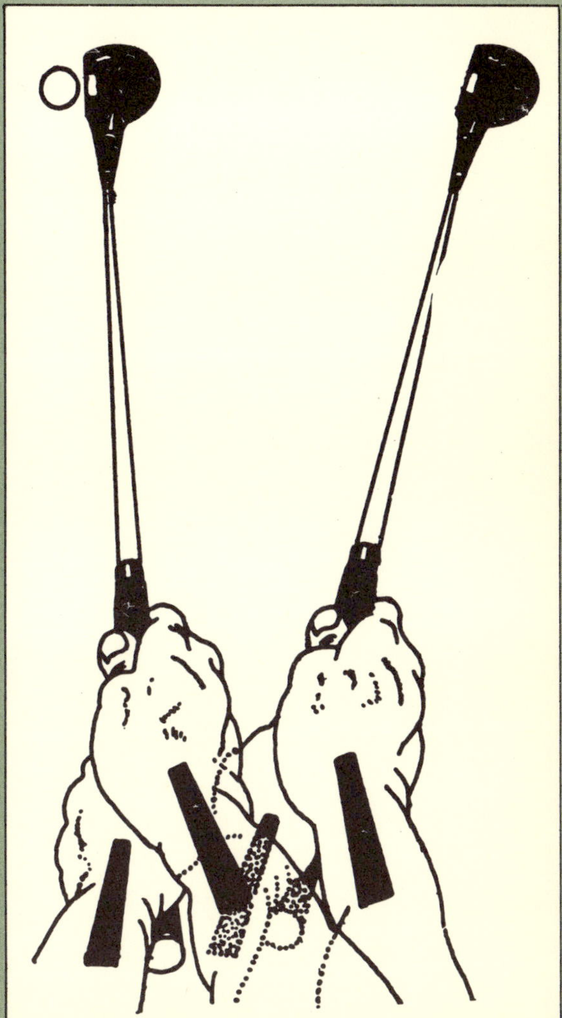

You should feel a good extension of your left side muscles as you swing the clubhead back. Unless you "use up" these muscles, you will not achieve maximum distance because your downswing will be cramped.

To promote this extension, always start the clubhead back as low as possible to the ground. This will lead to a wide backswing arc, with the left arm extended to keep the clubhead in position. The best way to do this is to feel you are more or less pushing the club back with your left hand. Your right hand and arm are passive at this point. Do not turn your wrists in any direction as you swing back.

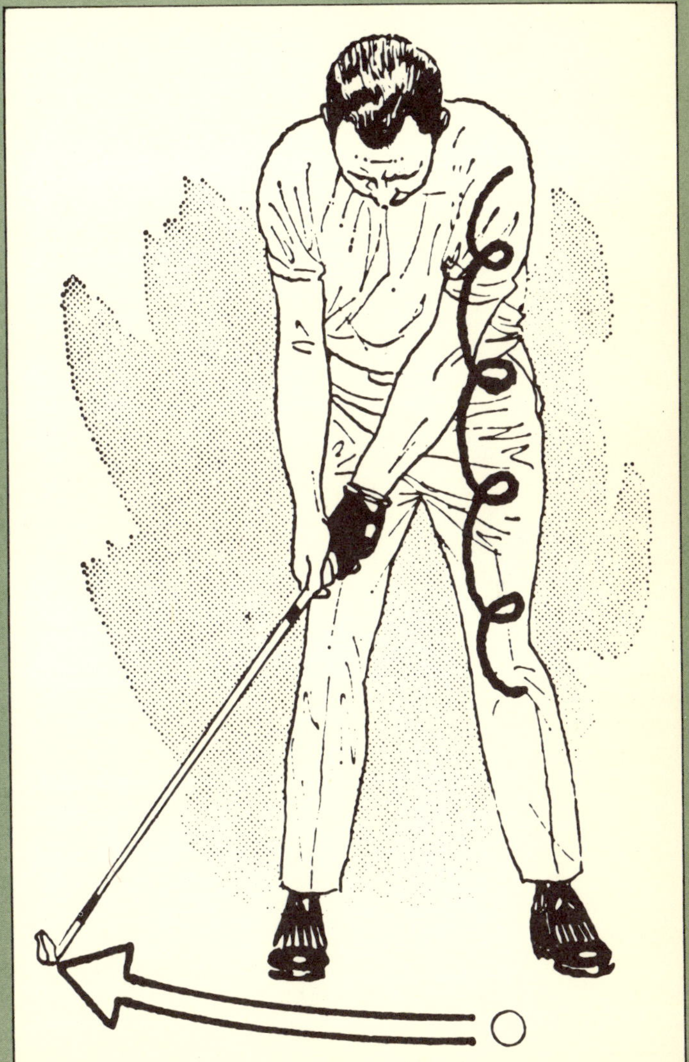

If the backswing arc isn't wide enough or is cramped, little upper body coiling power will be built up for later impact.

Begin your backswing with your left hand, arm and shoulder and move the clubhead back low to the ground. Don't use your wrists until you're past the halfway point in your backswing. If you feel your left side stretching, you're swinging correctly.

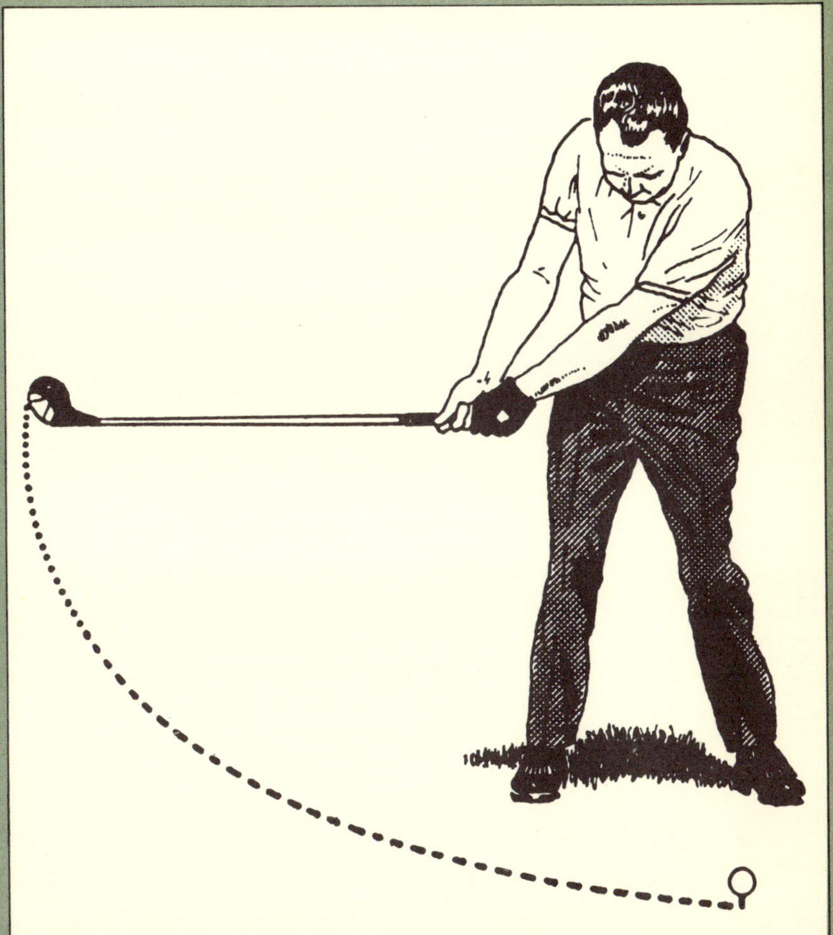

The left wrist and the back of the left forearm should form an essentially straight line (see illustration) at the top of the backswing.

When you achieve this, you have gone a long way toward keeping the clubface square to the intended line. That is, if the club is swung so that the shaft is horizontal to the ground at the top, the clubface should point up at about a 45-degree angle. All swings need not be that long, but the left wrist and forearm should always be straight at the top.

If the left wrist is convex, the face will be closed—pointing upward. If it's concave, the face will open—pointing more parallel to the ground.

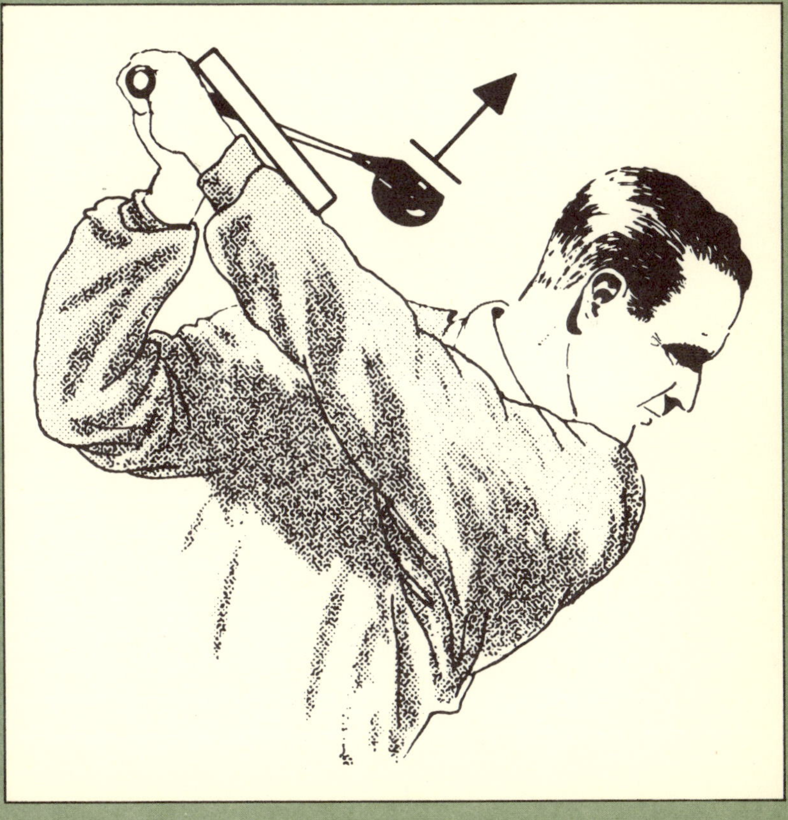

At the top of the backswing, the shaft should be on a plane parallel to the intended line. That position will give you your best shot.

If the shaft is pointing to the right of the target, you have swung back too far inside and you'll likely hook the ball to the left. If the shaft points to the left of the target, you'll probably slice to the right because you'll be swinging outside-in on the downswing.

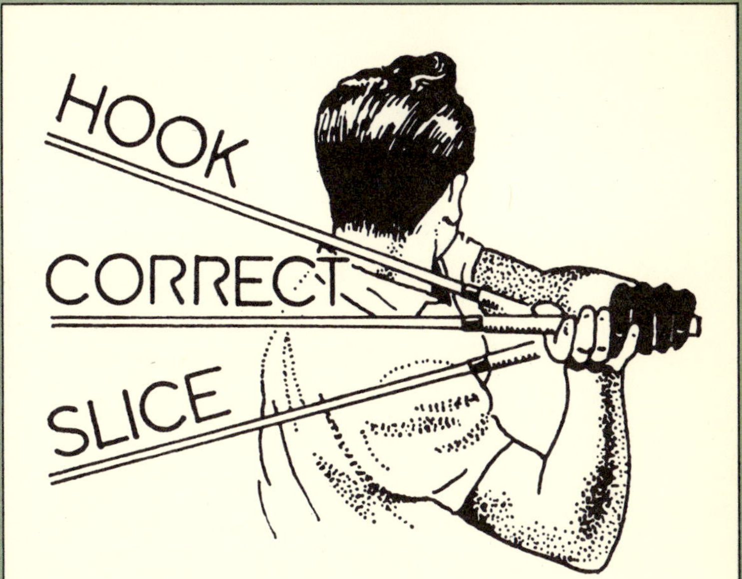
HOOK
CORRECT
SLICE

The Downswing

By using their hands and wrists too early, many golfers dissipate clubhead speed as they start the downswing. This will usually produce a weak swing in which the clubhead approaches the ball from outside the intended line, then cuts across and causes a slice.

If you will move as slowly as possible as you start the downswing and think about beginning your motion with your body and not your hands, you will retain wrist-cock achieved at the top of the backswing. The first downswing move should be a lateral slide of the hips toward the target, as illustrated. This places weight properly on the left side and will eventually lead to solid contact with the ball.

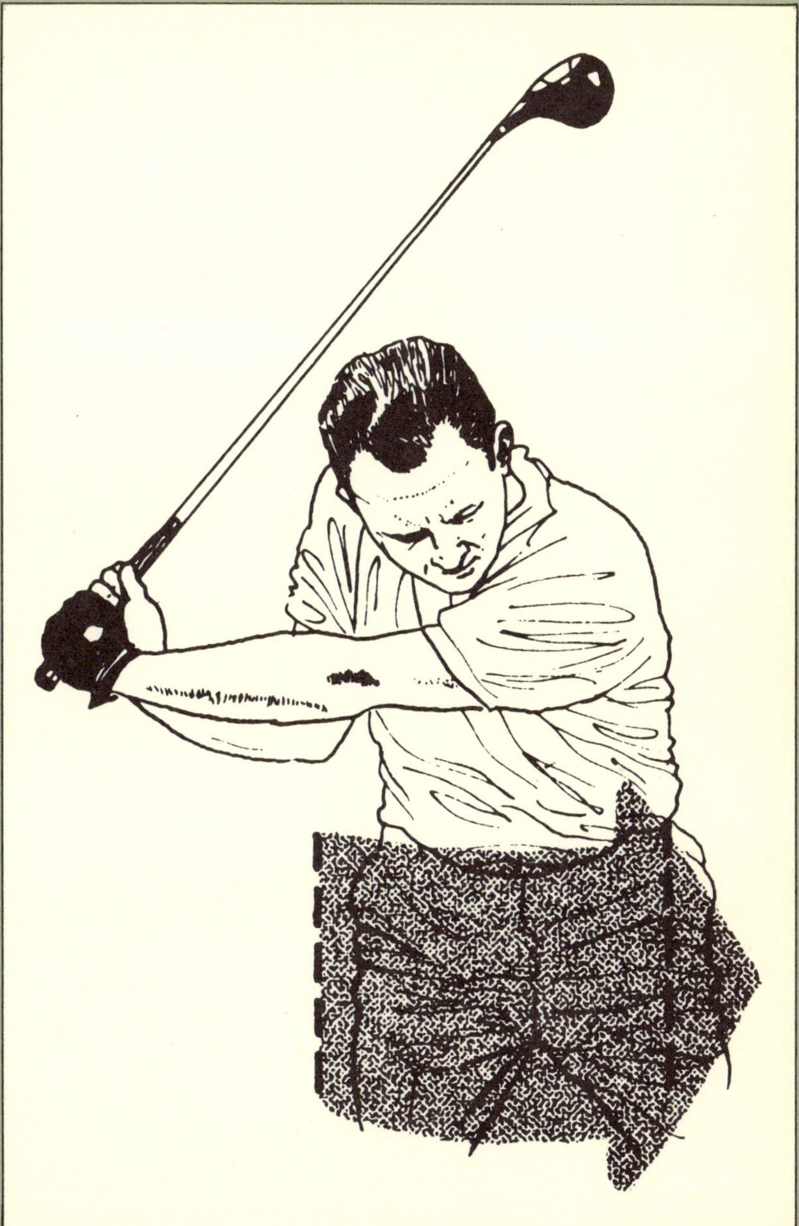

I slide my hips toward the target a bit at the start of the downswing. However, I do not let my upper body, especially including my head, move in that direction.

This sliding motion effectively moves a majority of my weight immediately to the left side as the downswing begins. If you feel the hip-slide is too difficult, merely plant the left heel solidly on the ground as the downswing begins (see illustration). Move your weight onto the left foot and swing "past" it, keeping your head in place.

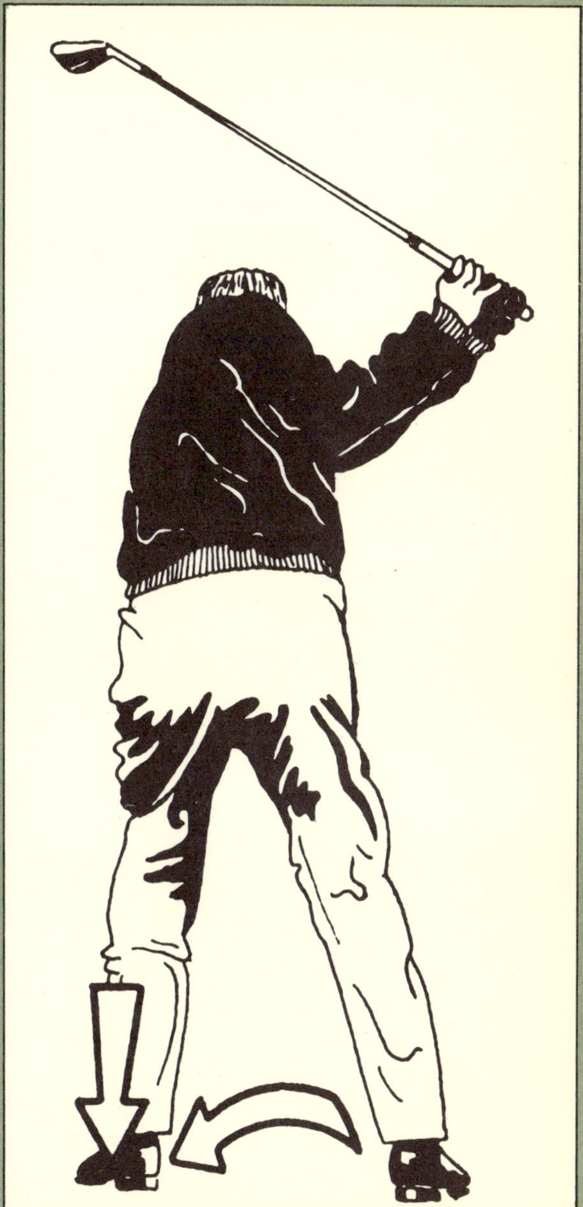

Throughout the swing the straight left arm keeps the clubhead in a constant arc, assuring your best chance of a square hit. If you extend your left arm at address and keep it straight as you swing back and down, you'll be able to get the club head squarely into the ball without too much trouble.

If you start with a straight left arm and then let it collapse, you may top the ball. If you start with it broken, you'll probably straighten at impact and hit "fat" shots.

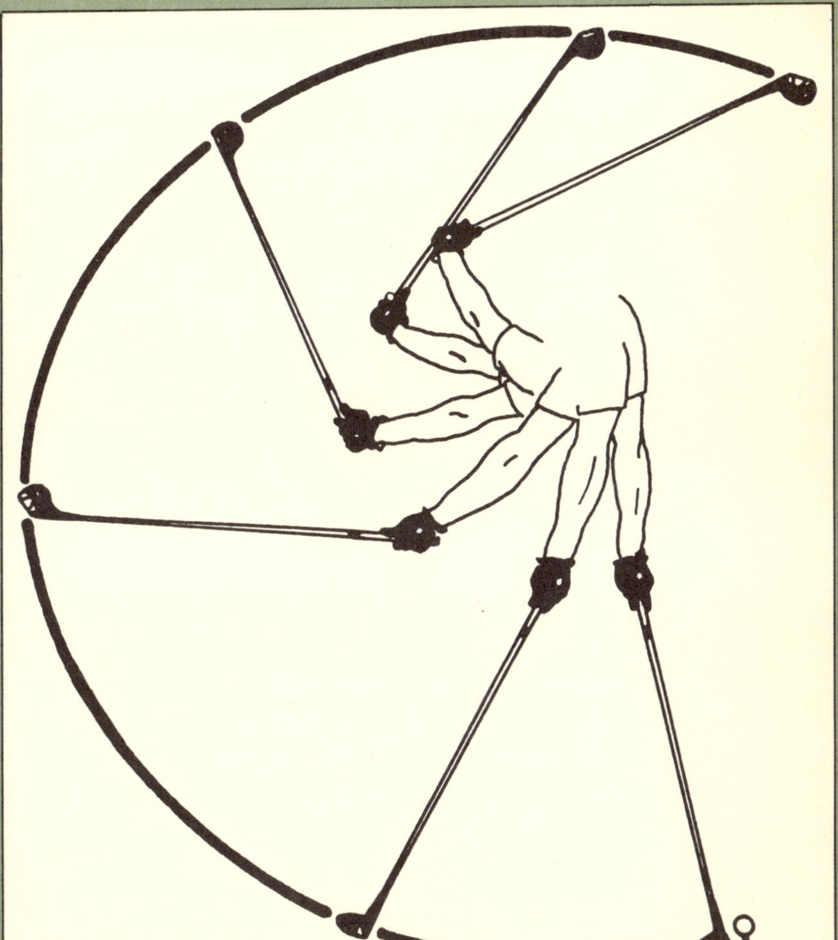

On the downswing, get your right side into the shot if you want to realize your power potential.

As you move into the impact area, you should have a feeling of "pushing off" with your right foot. Actually, this "pushing off" is concentrated in the toes, for the right heel has to come up if you're going to make a free move through the ball.

At the same time, your right knee moves in toward the target (see illustration). At impact, it should be pointing directly at the ball. This active right side motion effectively moves your weight to the left, where it belongs at impact.

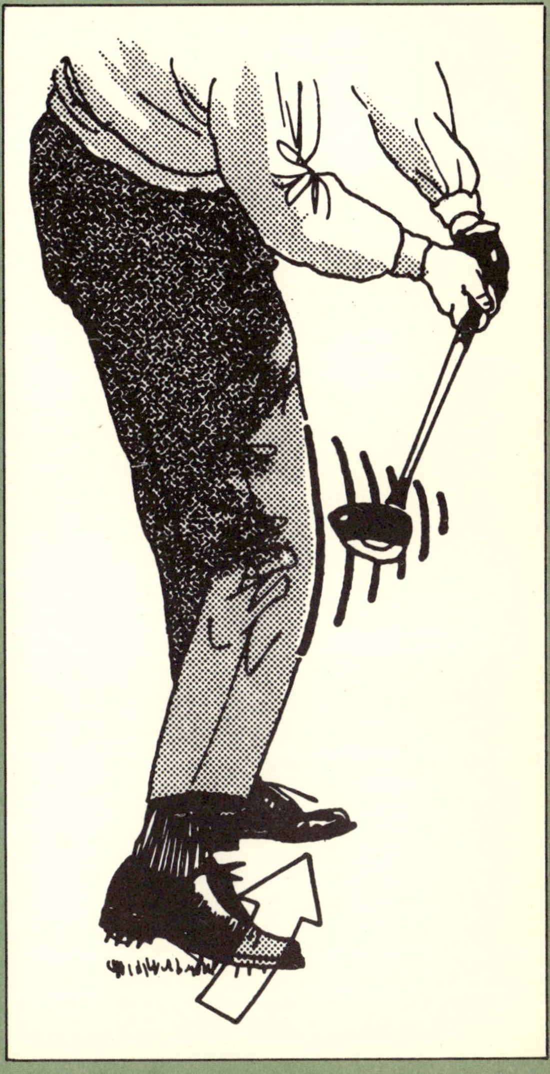

A most effective way of keeping the swing arc properly "inside" the target line is to move the right elbow in close to the body on the downswing.

There is no need to restrict moderate, right-elbow movement away from the body on the backswing. This might even help you to lengthen your swing arc. But once you start down, move that right elbow in close.

It stays there right through the impact area. Depending on your girth, it might even brush against your body as you strike the ball. When you do this, you'll get a square hit—you won't move the clubhead into the ball from the outside and slice to the right.

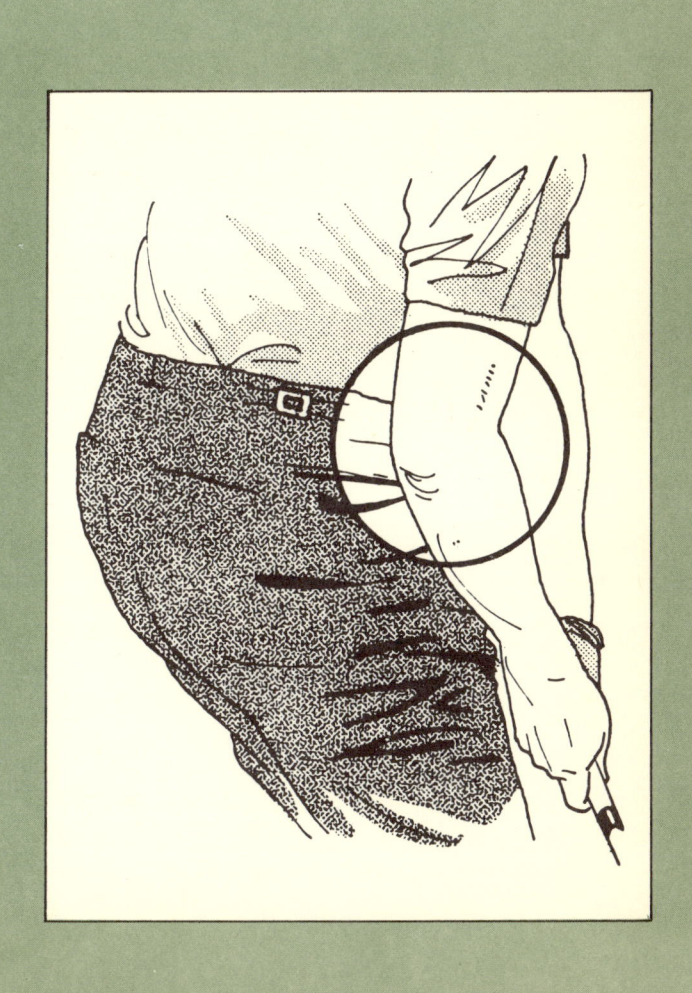

Just before impact, the wrists uncock and the clubhead is "released" into the ball.

To help maintain your wrist-cock before impact, start the downswing as slowly as possible and aim the butt end of the club at the ball, as illustrated. This will, in effect, keep the wrists cocked until the proper moment in the impact zone. You won't be tempted to "cast" the clubhead or start using your hands too early in the downswing.

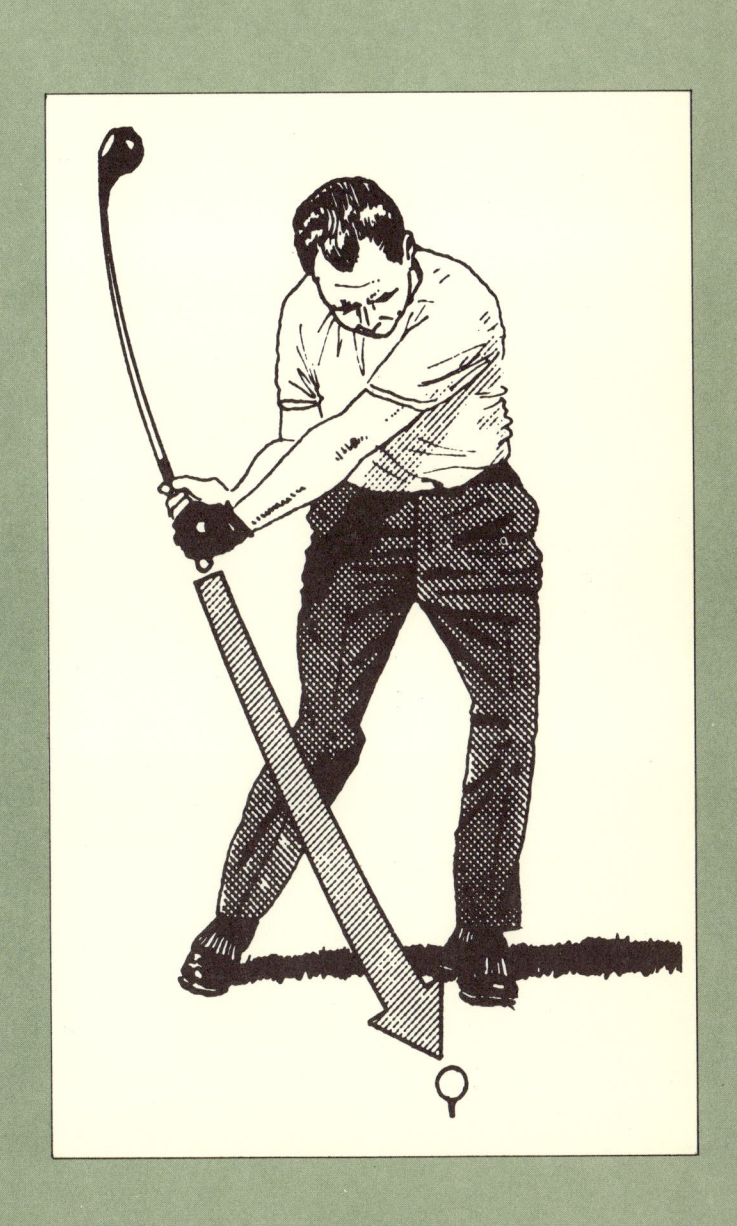

In the impact zone, the right elbow should move in close to the body. This is one thing that will keep the clubhead swinging down inside the intended line and help produce a square hit. The snug elbow starts at the beginning of the downswing. At that point, the right elbow should return to the right side, then stay in close until well after impact. If the right elbow moves away from the body at impact, the clubhead will approach the ball from outside the intended line and produce an off-line shot.

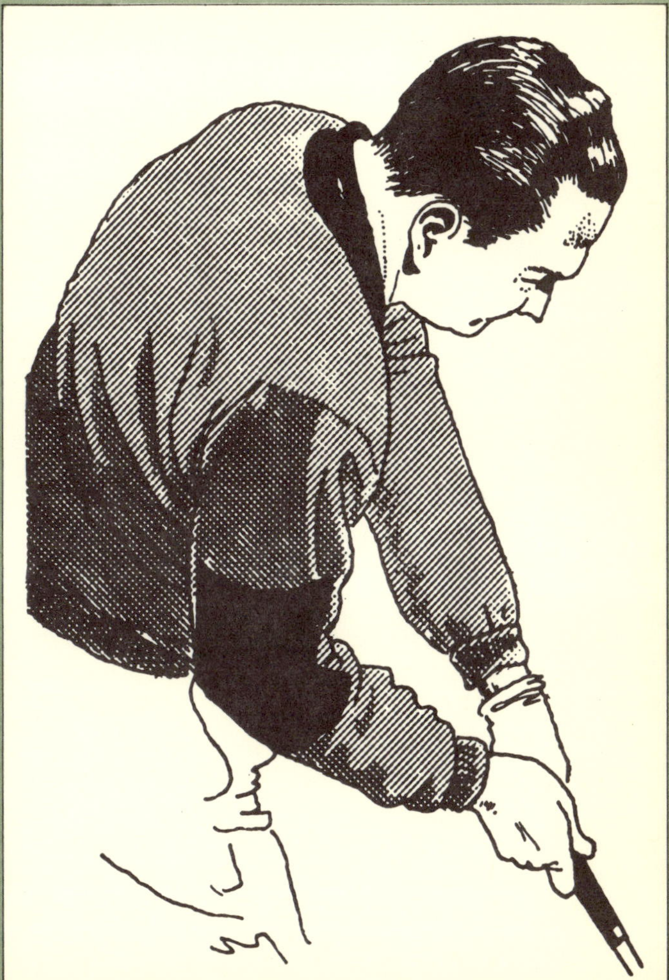

Accuracy is achieved by keeping the clubface absolutely square to the swing arc throughout the action. When this happens, the face is also square to the target at impact. A straight shot results.

The most important area in which the golfer should strive for this square face is at the beginning of the backswing.

Swing back with your left side, arm and hand providing impetus. Do not allow your hands to turn (pronate) in either direction as you move into the backswing. The best way to describe the hands at this point of the swing is "passive." Don't worry, they'll get into action later—but start out like this and you're well on the way to accuracy.

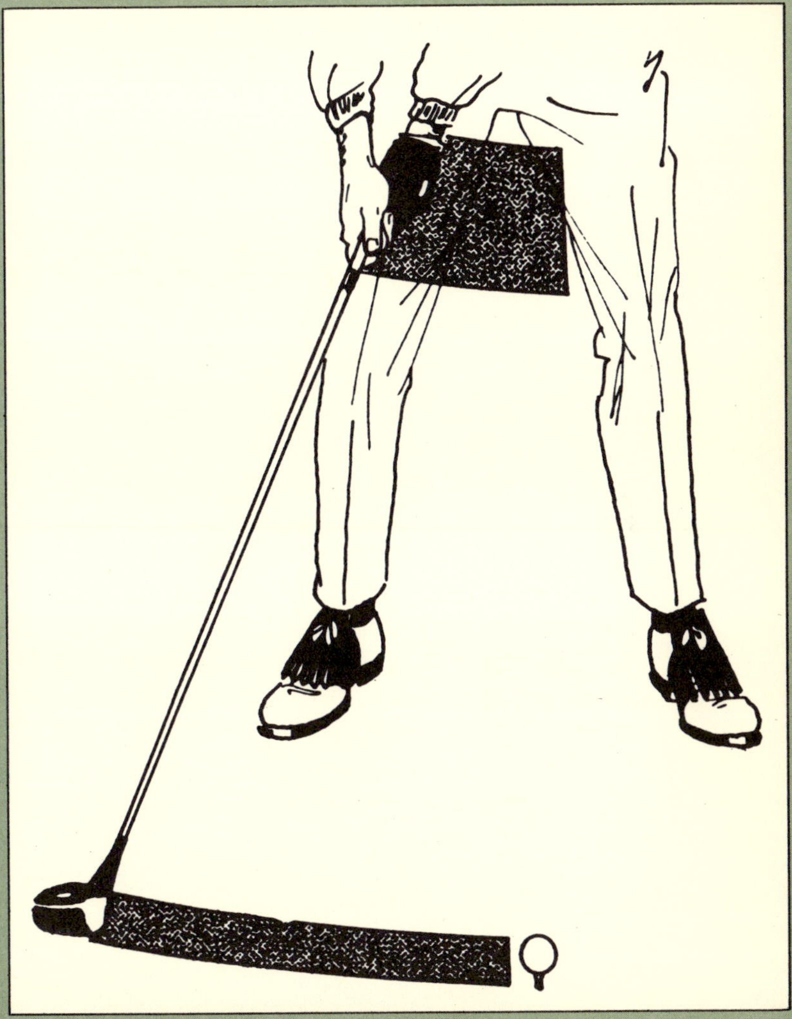

At impact, the hands must be ahead of the clubhead.

This is the position that puts power into the shot, for it enables the hands to slam through the ball with great force. If the hands lag behind the clubhead and ball at impact, a weak, uppercutting hit is the result.

Ideally, the left wrist should be bowed slightly toward the target at impact. It's a good idea to set yourself that way at address by a toward-the-target shift of your hands, then holding them that way back and through.

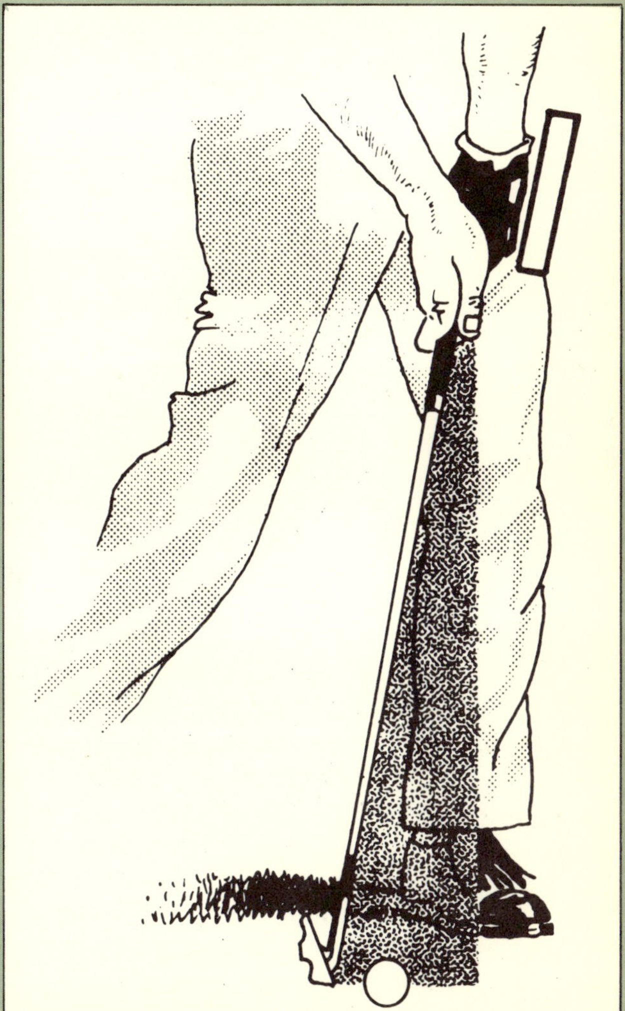

At impact, the best shots result from a very firm left side. The left wrist, especially, should not be allowed to collapse. When this happens, the clubhead passes the hands in a little flipping motion that will kill any shot's power.

Allow the left hand and wrist to lead the clubhead into and a little past the ball's original position. The back of the left hand should move toward the target. This squares the clubface and keeps it that way long enough to send the ball in the desired direction.

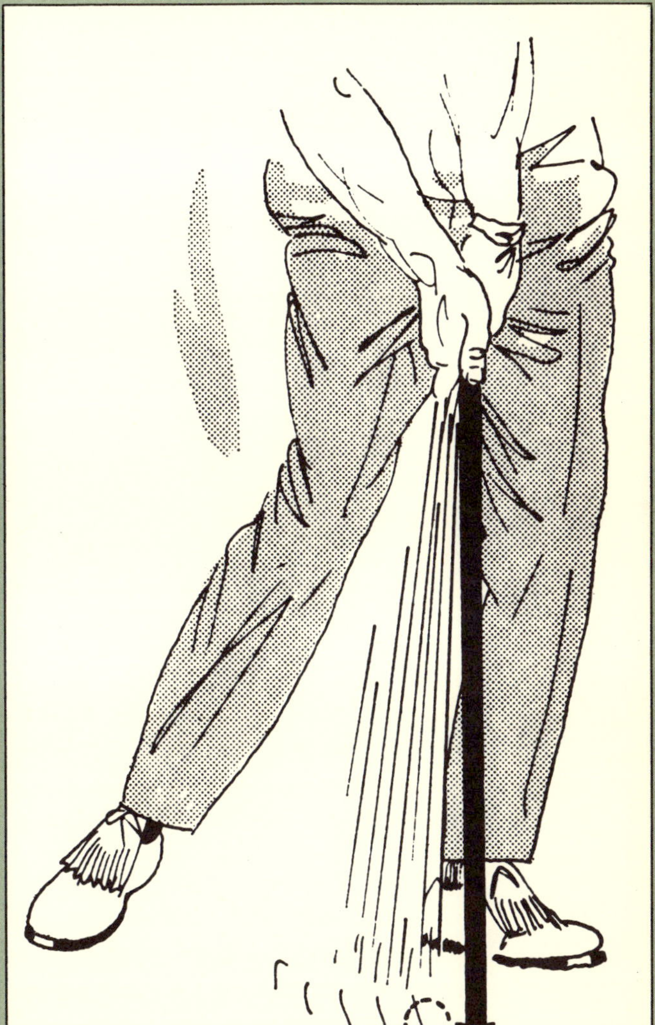

An indication of a properly-active right side is the position of the right knee. As you drive into the ball, the right knee should flex inward, toward the target. When this happens, your body falls into good hitting position—as long as the left side holds firm.

As your right knee moves more and more toward the target, you should come up a bit on the inside of your right foot and feel a definite surge of power from the right side.

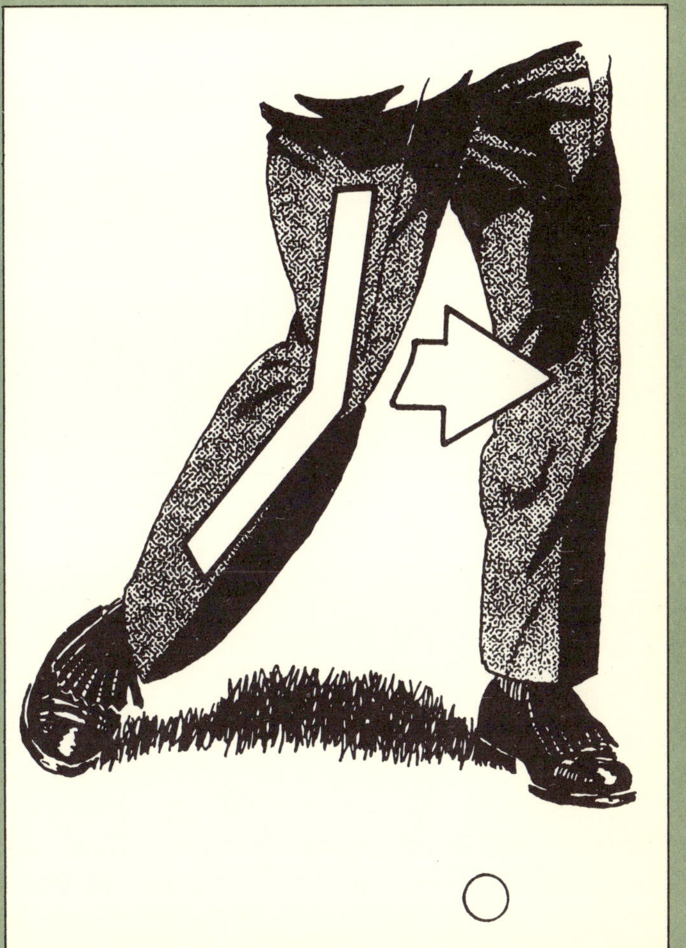

Some golfers move the upper body toward the target in the impact area. This will reduce power, for it serves to slow down the clubhead at this important point. Clubhead speed is what produces power and distance.

As you begin the downswing, move your weight quickly to your left side. Swing your right shoulder down and under, past your chin. These actions will help keep your upper body properly behind the ball at impact. You'll get that accelerating whip into the ball that will never happen if you allow your head and shoulders to move past the ball toward the target.

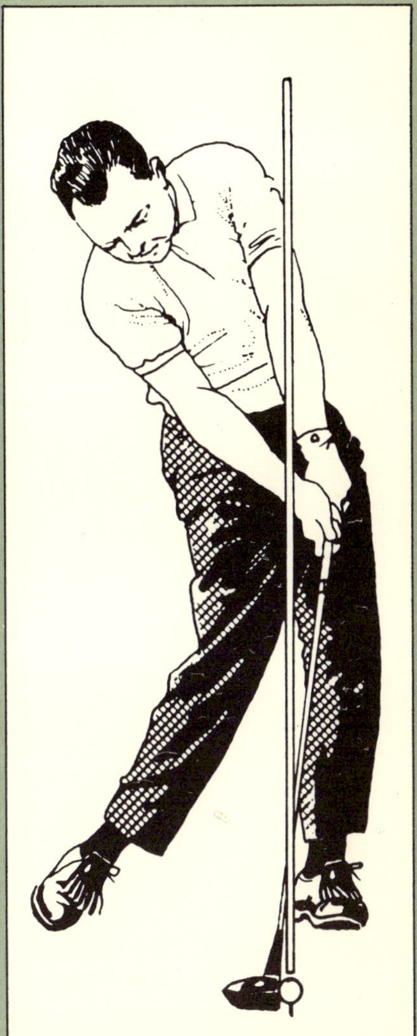

Are you raising or somehow altering the path of the clubhead "through" the ball so that you are not getting a solid hit?

If so, perhaps this tip would help. After every iron shot from a normal lie, simply watch for the divot to appear before you allow your eyes to raise and follow the flight of the ball. The knowledge that you intend to do this will automatically help you stay with the shot longer and will give you more solid contact with the ball.

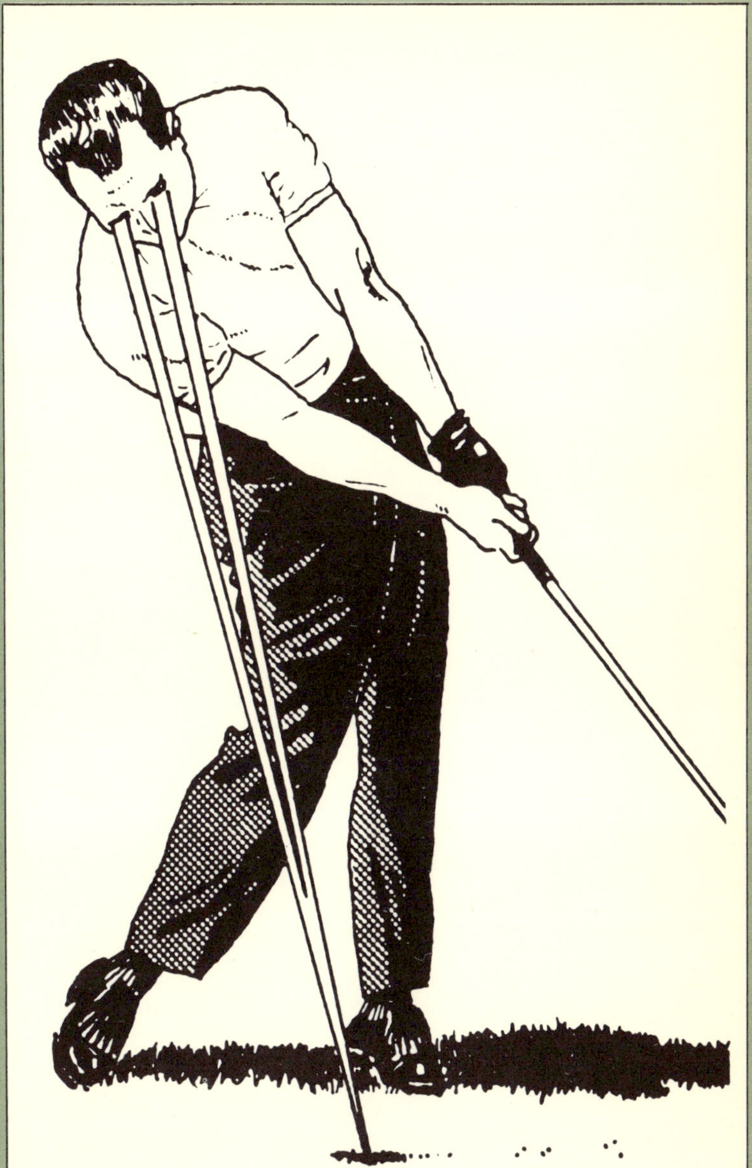

Every golfer has heard that he must keep his head still to swing with the greatest effectiveness. This is essentially true, but there is a danger in overemphasizing this point.

Should you strive to keep your head absolutely stationary, chances are you will bind up your neck muscles, which, in turn, injects unwanted tension throughout the body.

This would especially affect the downswing. Those who keep the head down too long after impact will probably have slowed their action well before the ball is struck. Get the feeling that your head is gradually pivoting as you hit. Your eyes can safely leave the ball's original position when your hands reach about shoulder-high in the follow-through.

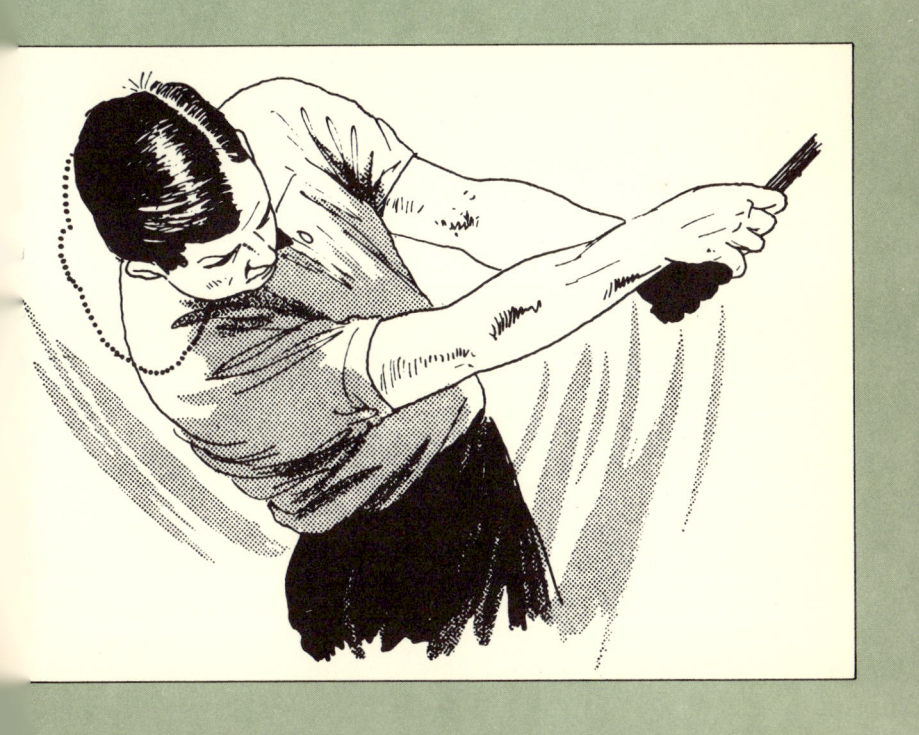

A roundhouse swing of the shoulders on the downswing will usually bring the clubhead into the ball in a slicing arc—from outside the intended line.

The shoulders should actually tilt rather vertically. How much depends on how tall you are—the taller you are, the more vertically your shoulders will tilt; shorter players can swing their shoulders on a more horizontal plane.

In all cases, however, the right shoulder should pass under the chin as and after the ball is struck. This serves to square up the clubface and move the clubhead directly into the ball, producing the straightest shots.

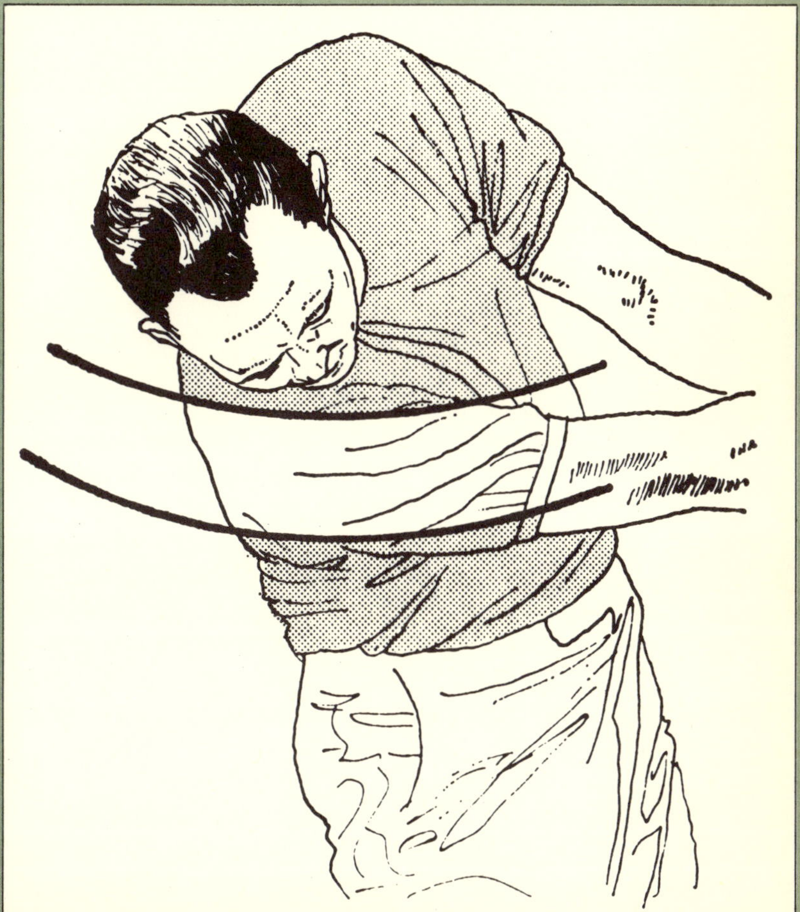

Especially under pressure, any golfer may try to "steer" the ball to its objective. Chances are, this won't work. For one thing, it makes for an "anxious," jerky and inhibited swing in which the golfer does not move smoothly. He's in a hurry to see where the ball goes and may raise his head and body too soon, causing a topped shot. Because his muscles are moving hesitantly, they won't be extended and impact is not likely to be solid. All of this is often indicated by a short finish.

Once you determine how you want to swing to get to your specified target, step up to the ball and swing away without hesitation. You'll extend your muscles, you'll swing more smoothly—and you'll get a better shot. If you do this, you'll finish with your weight balanced easily on your left side.

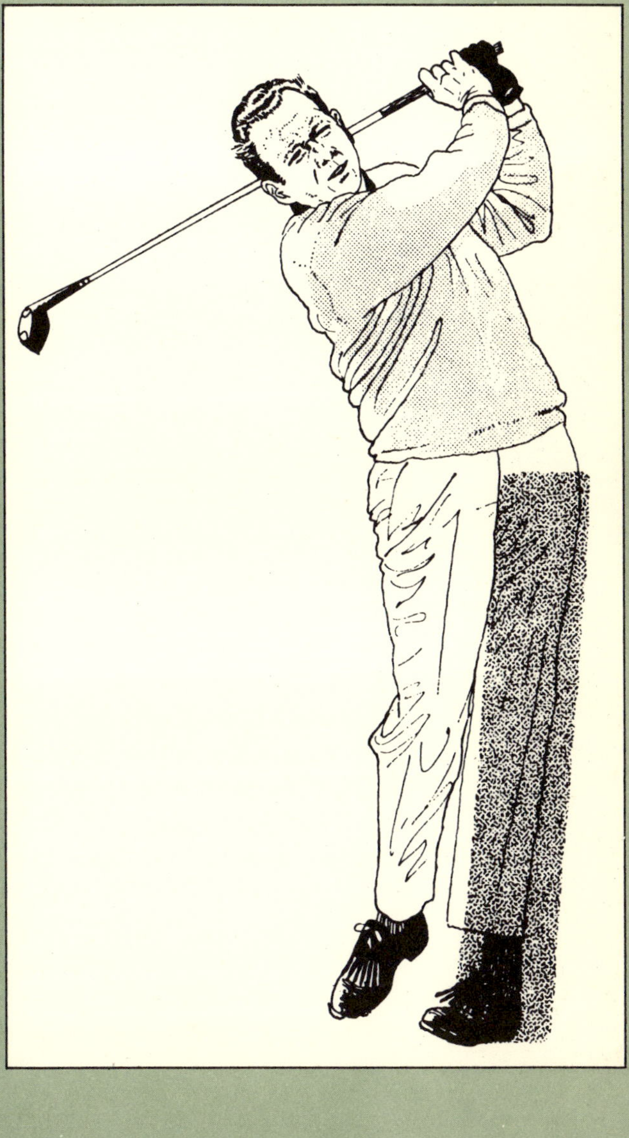

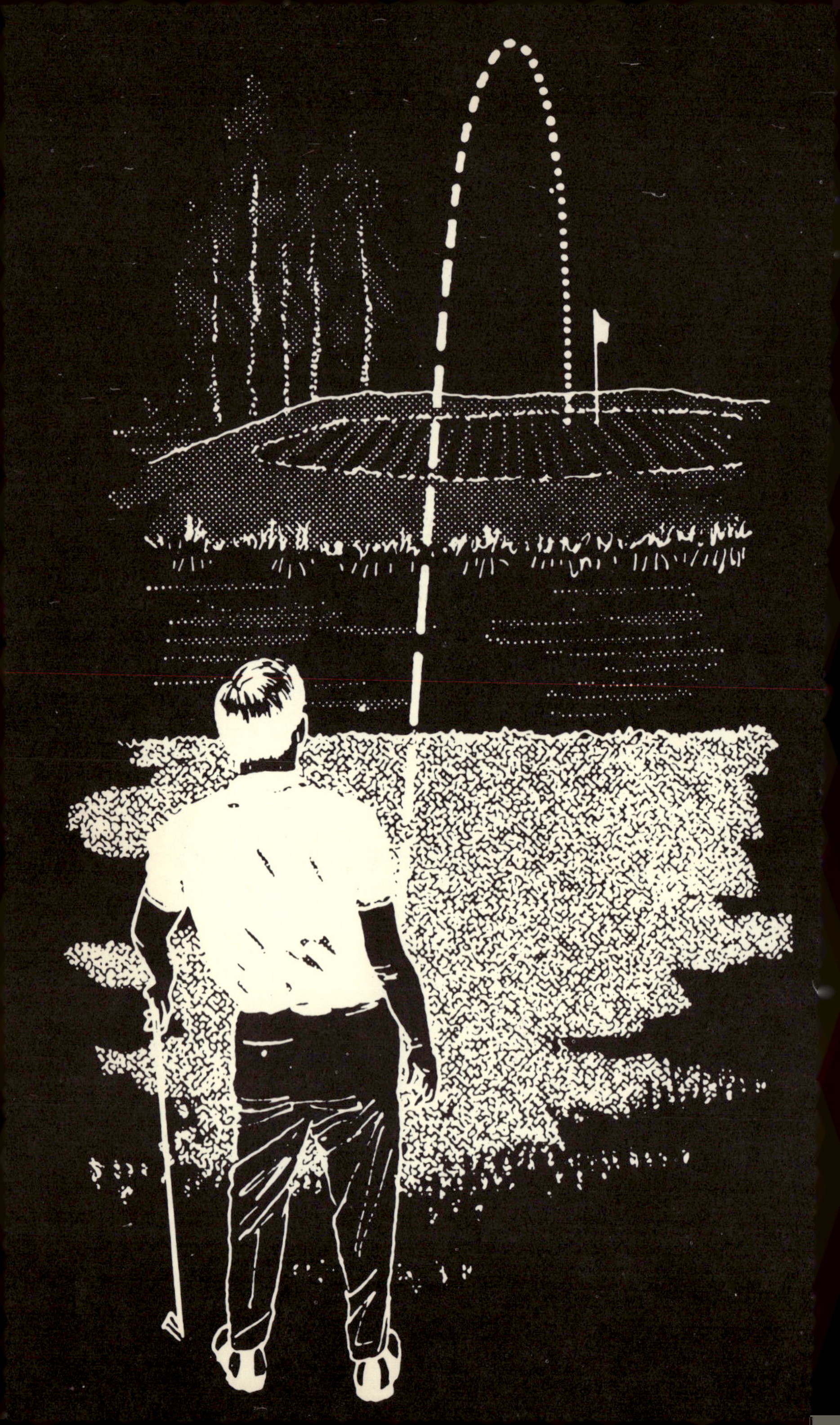

Fairway Shots

Many average golfers are uncomfortable using woods on the fairway and, faced with a long shot to the green, frequently turn to an iron. This is due to unfamiliarity with the club and the assignment. I would suggest to all golfers that they try to gain confidence in fairway woods, particularly the No. 3 wood.

Most pros, limited in the number of clubs they may carry in the bag, pass up the brassie, or the No. 2 wood, in preference for the No. 3 and No. 4 woods. Their reasoning is simple. The brassie has little more loft than the driver. With a good lie in the fairway, they can hit a driver as well as a brassie. With a risky lie, they would rather go with the No. 3 wood.

The greater the loft, the safer the club. I think the No. 3 wood is the most serviceable wood club in the bag. You don't get the distance you can get with the driver but you get greater accuracy.

In some cases—the exceptions being the

long par four holes and the par fives that may be reached in two—it may be just as practical, for safety's sake, to hit a No. 3 wood off the tee. Many of the pros do it when the fairways look like gun barrels or they must thread the ball through fairway bunkers.

The Irons

The irons may be broken into three categories—the Nos. 2, 3 and 4 irons are the long irons for distances ranging from 210 down to 160 yards. The middle irons—5, 6 and 7—go from 165 yards to 130. The short irons—8, 9 and the wedge—run from 130 for a weak-hit No. 8 to 40 yards for the gentlest assignment of the wedge, which may be used for any shot up to 100 yards. These are the distances of the pros, but even they vary according to the strength and hitting power of the individual.

Whereas Nicklaus may average 165 or 170 yards with a 5 iron, Deane Beman, who is much slighter and less long on all of his shots, probably could get no more than 140 yards with the same club. All of this is immaterial. The point I wish to make is that the average golfer—and sometimes the tournament pro—often tries to squeeze the ultimate out of a certain club when he could get the job done much more satisfactorily by choosing a larger club and not exerting himself.

As mentioned before, I normally swing with about 80 per cent of my power. It is possible for me to hit a seven-iron 170 yards. But to do so is self-defeating. It requires full strength. I would be smarter to pick a six-iron or perhaps even a five-iron, swing easier and rely on the percentages.

Most average golfers make the mistake of judging themselves by yardage charts which they see in golf books and magazine instructional pieces. These charts are usually drawn up by averaging the distance of the pros. The average golfer may look at a chart and see that No. 4 iron should be hit about 175 yards. He will come to a hole, find himself faced with that distance and immediately ask the caddie for a No. 4 iron. Chances are he will be well short. The shot, for him, may be either a No. 3 or a No. 2.

The trouble is that most golfers are following the wrong charts. They would be wise to study their own capabilities and on the basis of this draw up their own charts. This can be done quite easily. Granting they play once a week, they should learn just how far they can hit a ball with the various clubs and then, with the help perhaps of their caddies, should formulate their own set of guide-lines.

Once this is done, I would recommend that these golfers take an additional step.

If the survey shows that a player can hit a six-iron, let us say, 140 yards when he is going all out, then that distance should be marked down as a five-iron assignment.

Remember the cardinal rule: Swing easy, swing well within yourself and score better.

The golfer should have a complete file—mental if not written—of the special action of every club in the bag, not only how far he can hit it, but also how high, with what trajectory and what spin. Once equipped with this information, he will find golf not only easier but more enjoyable.

It is said—only half facetiously—that the modern golfer buys his shots from the manufacturer. He doesn't have to gauge or finesse the shot. This is done by the club. Regardless of whether you hit a straight-faced iron, which goes lower and farther, or the deep-faced clubs, which fly higher but for less distance, the swing is the same. Thus, you only have to decide which is the proper club for the particular assignment. The club itself—with its varying degrees of loft—does the job.

I say this is theory, and only partly correct. It is true that the grip is the same. The technique is unchanged. There is the same address and there is little or no difference in the tempo of the swing. The policy of the swing remains the same—swing easily and don't press.

In running the full gamut of the irons,

there is definitely a change in the stance. The longer the iron the wider the stance, because the longer the iron the longer also the shaft. Whereas the feet are positioned about the width of the shoulders for a five-iron, they are placed closer together for the nine-iron or the wedge. Relatively, the left foot is withdrawn a bit. This takes some of the left side out of the shot on short irons and gets the ball in the air better.

Even with the manufacture of superbly fashioned and sensitized clubs, the golfer cannot become a mere automaton. He must think. He must choose. Golf is still a game of decisions. Execution becomes simpler as practice, dedication and experience escalate. Judgment, poise and concentration still go into the making of the good golf shot.

Fairway Shots

You should assess every shot, even the putt, from behind the ball before you assume your stance. Sometimes the target will look a lot different from your address position than it really is. But from behind the ball, the "picture" is true.

As you walk to the ball, get it between you and your target. Pause a moment to imagine just how you would like the ball to fly. Get in mind what club you will need for the shot and how you want to swing.

Once this is all decided, you'll be ready for good swing execution as you step up to the ball. You won't have to worry about where you want the ball to go—you'll know, and this is conducive to hitting it exactly to that point.

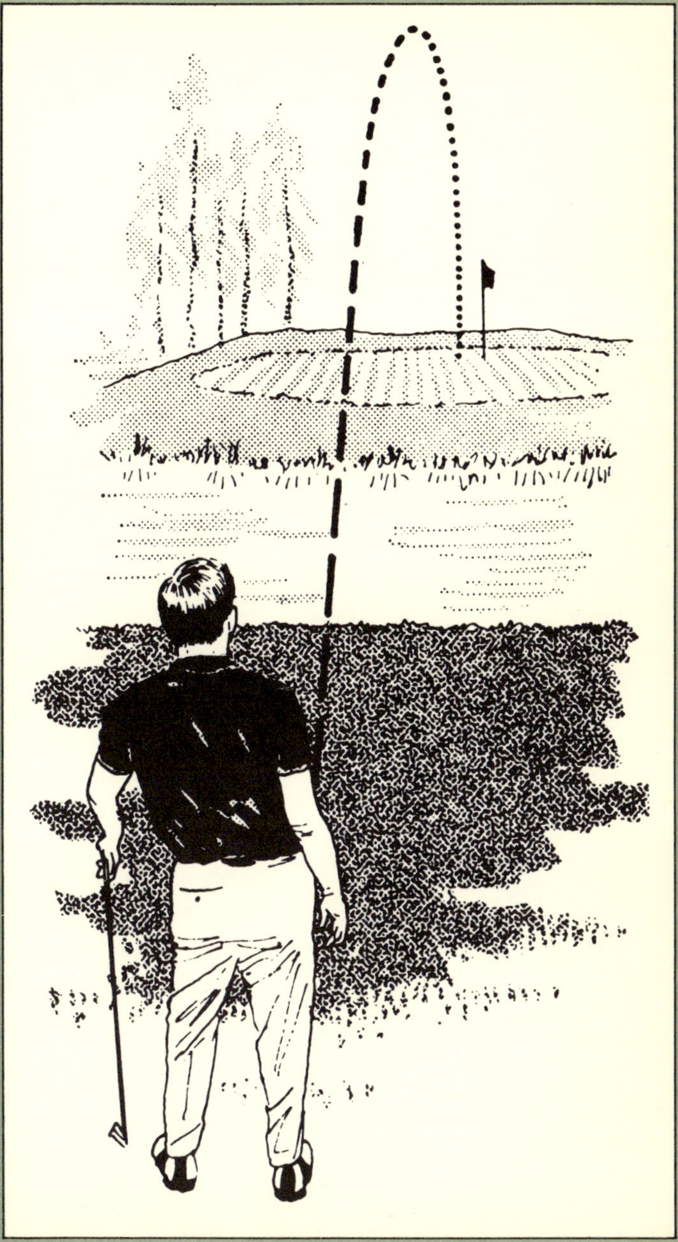

Tension hurts many a golfer's game. It tightens muscles, especially those around the back of the neck, and makes a smooth swing an impossibility.

No matter what the pressure, try to move into position for every shot in a relaxed, unhurried manner. (Some players find it especially helpful to take a couple of deep breaths while they are settling into their stance.) Consciously relax your arm muscles, especially those in the forearms, by waggling the clubhead over the ball a few times.

When you have mentally and physically drained away tension, you're ready to make your best pass at the ball.

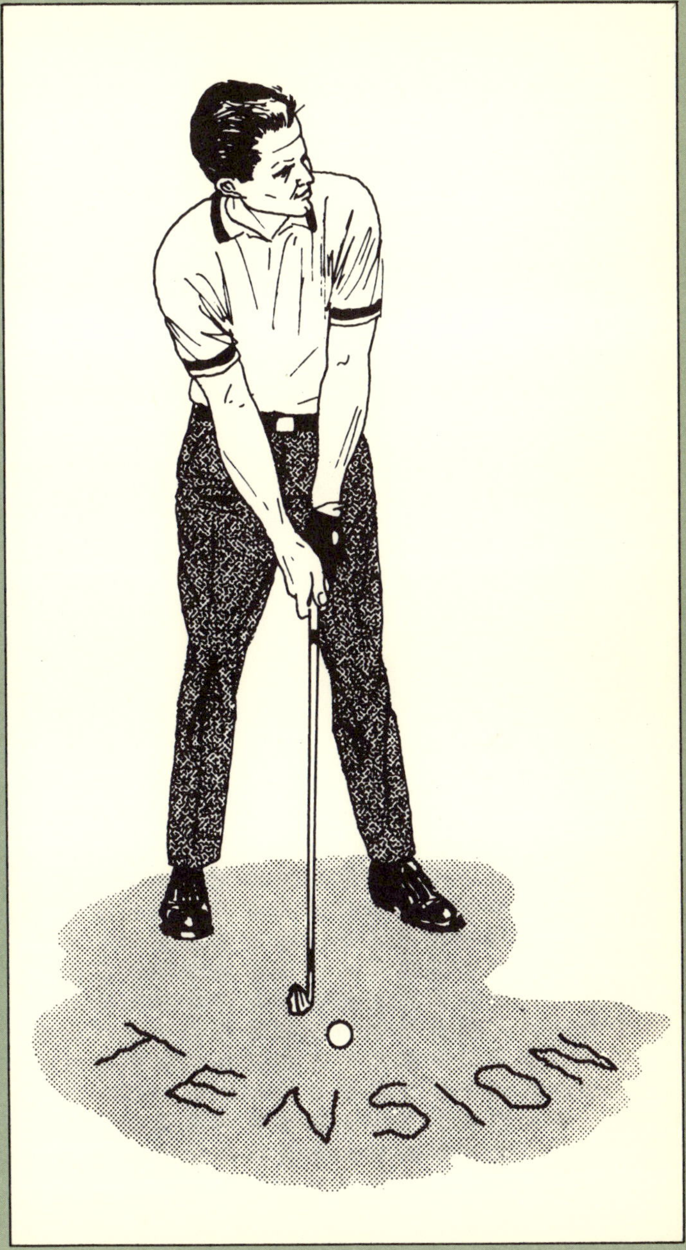
TENSION

For long shots from light-to-medium rough, many golfers automatically reach for an iron, but sometimes they are unnecessarily sacrificing distance. Try a 4-wood. Its head will cut through quite a bit of grass. It's heavier, so you don't have to swing as hard. The longer shaft of the wood also helps produce a wider swing arc than an iron.

Play the ball off the left heel and open the clubface and stance a bit (see illustration). Stand a little closer to the ball than usual so you produce an upright swing arc. Break your wrists a little more quickly than usual on the backswing and swing directly down at the ball.

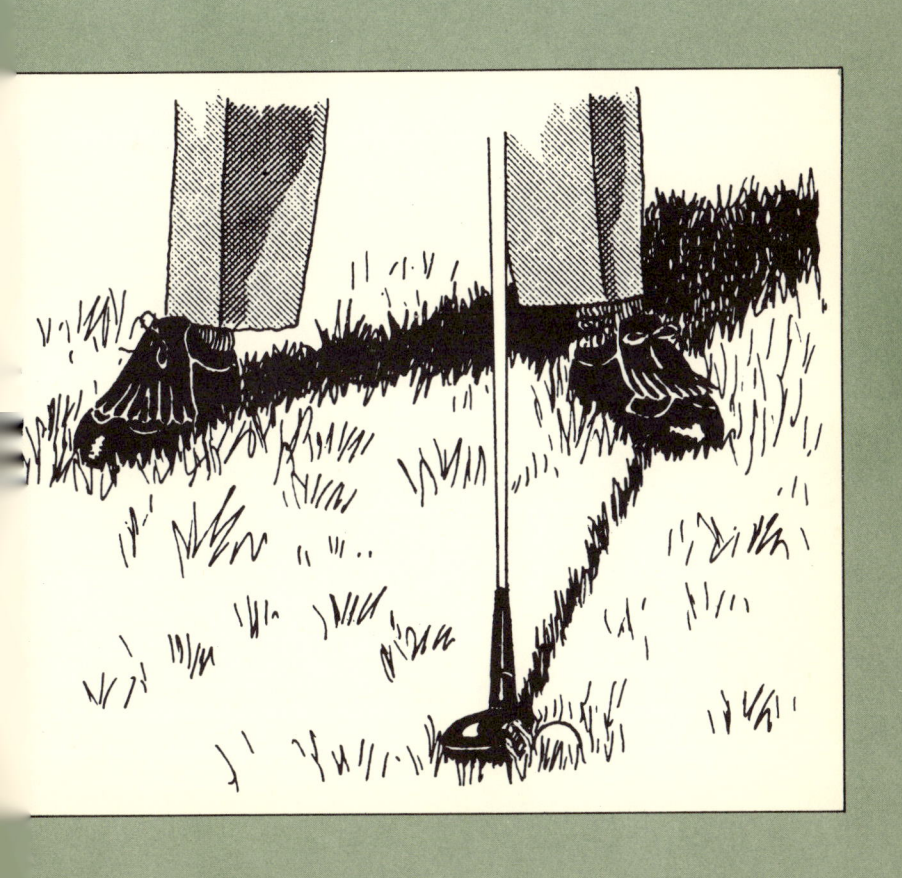

Knowing how far you can hit your various irons is a great confidence-builder. When you know you can hit a given iron for a certain number of yards, the door opens to a fine shot.

The place to determine your iron lengths is in practice. Have definite targets when you use them on the range. During play, figure out landmarks along the course that you can use to gauge the yardage to the greens.

Following is a chart of usual distances achieved by a middle-handicapper. Yours may differ, but you could use this as an initial guide:

Club	Distance	Club	Distance
2-iron	180-190	6-iron	140-150
3-iron	170-180	7-iron	130-140
4-iron	160-170	8-iron	120-130
5-iron	150-160	9-iron	110-120

3-IRON	✚	170 YARDS
5-IRON	✚	150 YARDS
7-IRON	✚	130 YARDS

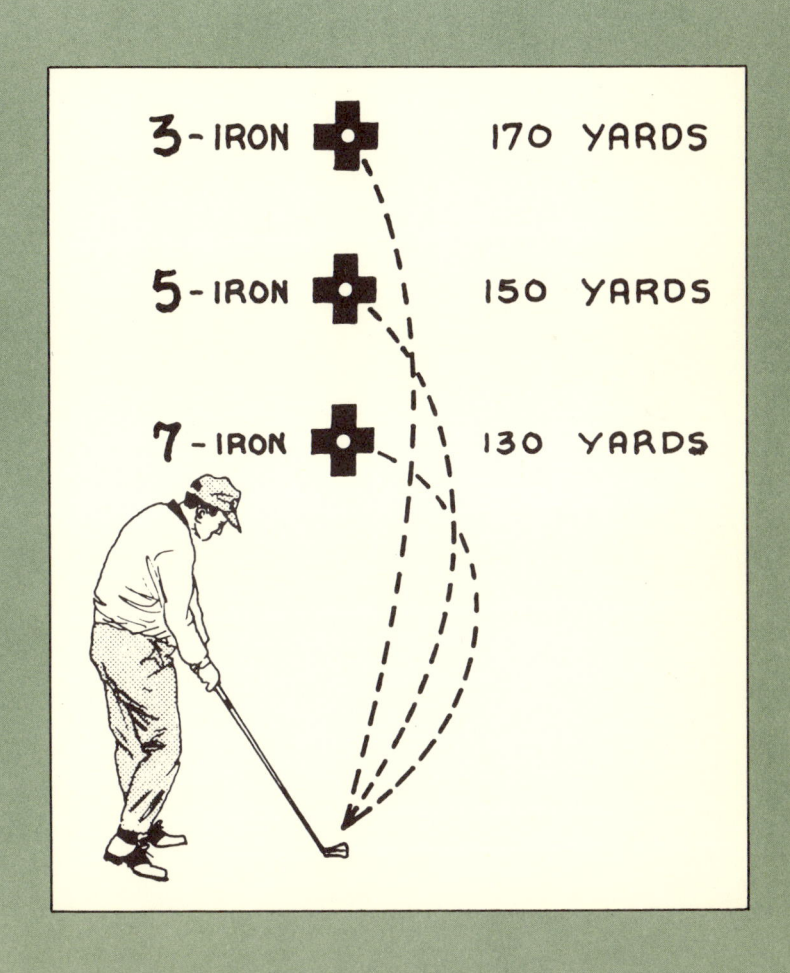

Long irons (the 2, 3 and 4) are especially helpful on holes where you need good length and accuracy. Properly struck, a long iron shot will have enough backspin to stick on the green after a few bounces. And such shots aren't as likely as fairway woods to zoom out of control.

The long iron swing is more of a sweep than an abrupt, direct hit. Keep this in mind when you step up to such a shot. Position your hands even with the ball at address so you don't take any natural loft off the clubface. Make a full, rhythmic backswing, with good extension of the left arm, and be certain to contact the ball first with an active "release" of the hands and wrists. You can't baby this shot.

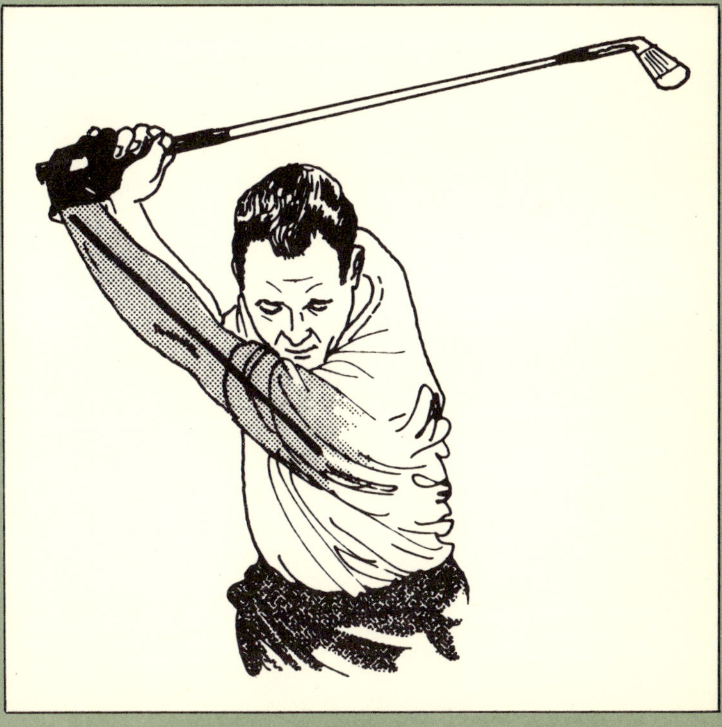

Every golfer, sooner or later, finds it necessary to hit shots other than the usual ones. The draw or hook, in which the ball follows a right-to-left pattern, is one of these. Shots such as this should be learned in practice so that they will come easily in actual play.

To hook the ball, it is necessary to put a counterclockwise spin on it. This is achieved by moving the clubhead into the ball from well inside the intended line, then out to the right for a brief moment and finally back inside, as illustrated.

Use a closed stance, with the right foot withdrawn from the intended line more than the left. Position the ball in the front half of your stance, and the clubface so that it points at the eventual target. On the downswing, keep your right elbow close into your body.

TO TARGET

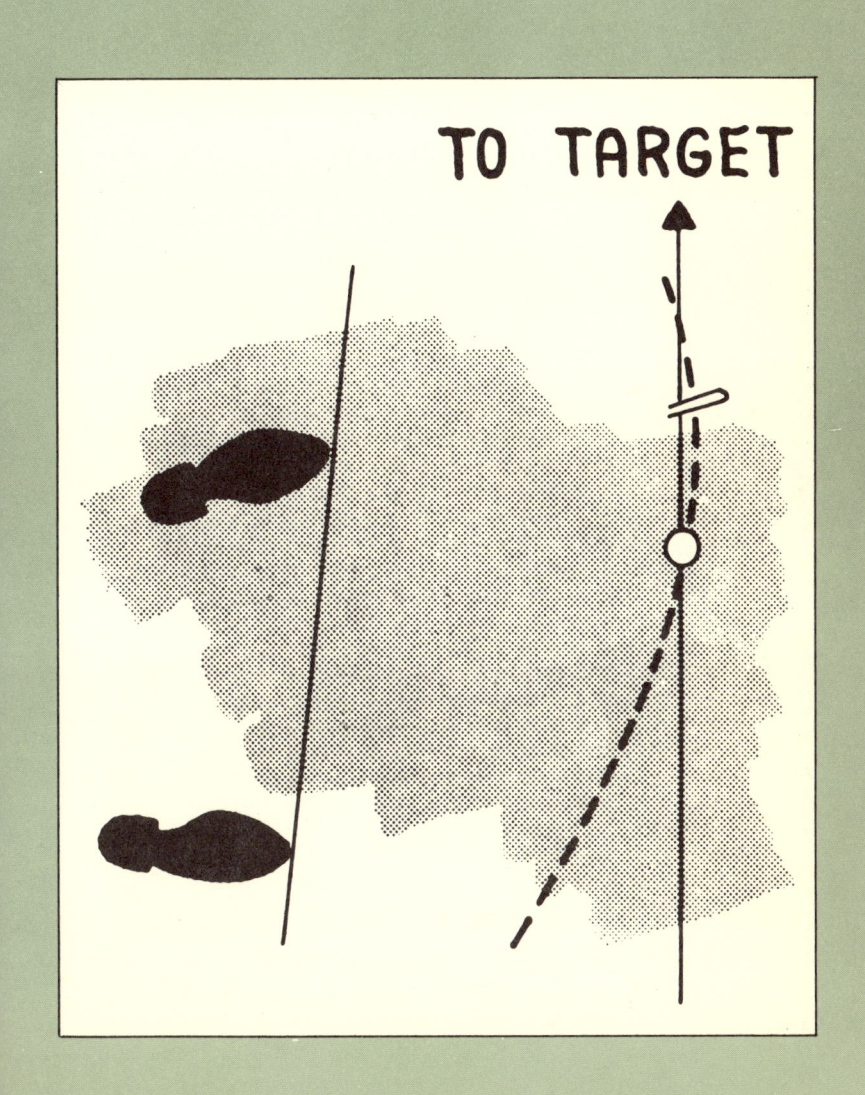

Sometimes the difficulty you have from long irons stems from where you play the ball at address. The shafts on these clubs (2 and 3 irons) are relatively long, so the ball ought to be played fairly well forward—about an inch inside the left heel. This gives you room to take a good, full-bodied swipe at the ball. When the ball is played farther back, the swing tends to get cramped and that won't work with these clubs.

Another good point is to position your hands over the ball at address, not behind it. If you do the latter, you will decrease the loft of the clubface and find it difficult to get the ball airborne.

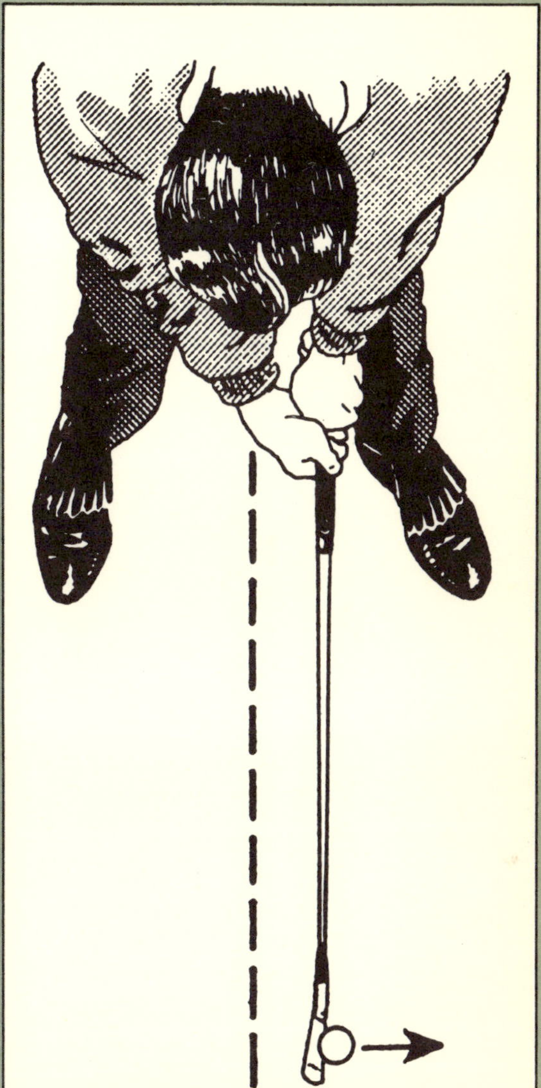

Simple as it may seem, many golfers hook or pull their long irons because they have the clubface incorrectly positioned at address. An optical illusion can cause this.

To be truly square to your target, see that the bottom line of the clubface is exactly perpendicular to the target line, as illustrated. The hook or pull is caused when golfers incorrectly align the top of the iron clubhead square to the target. This causes the face to actually close and point to the left, and results in the off-line shot.

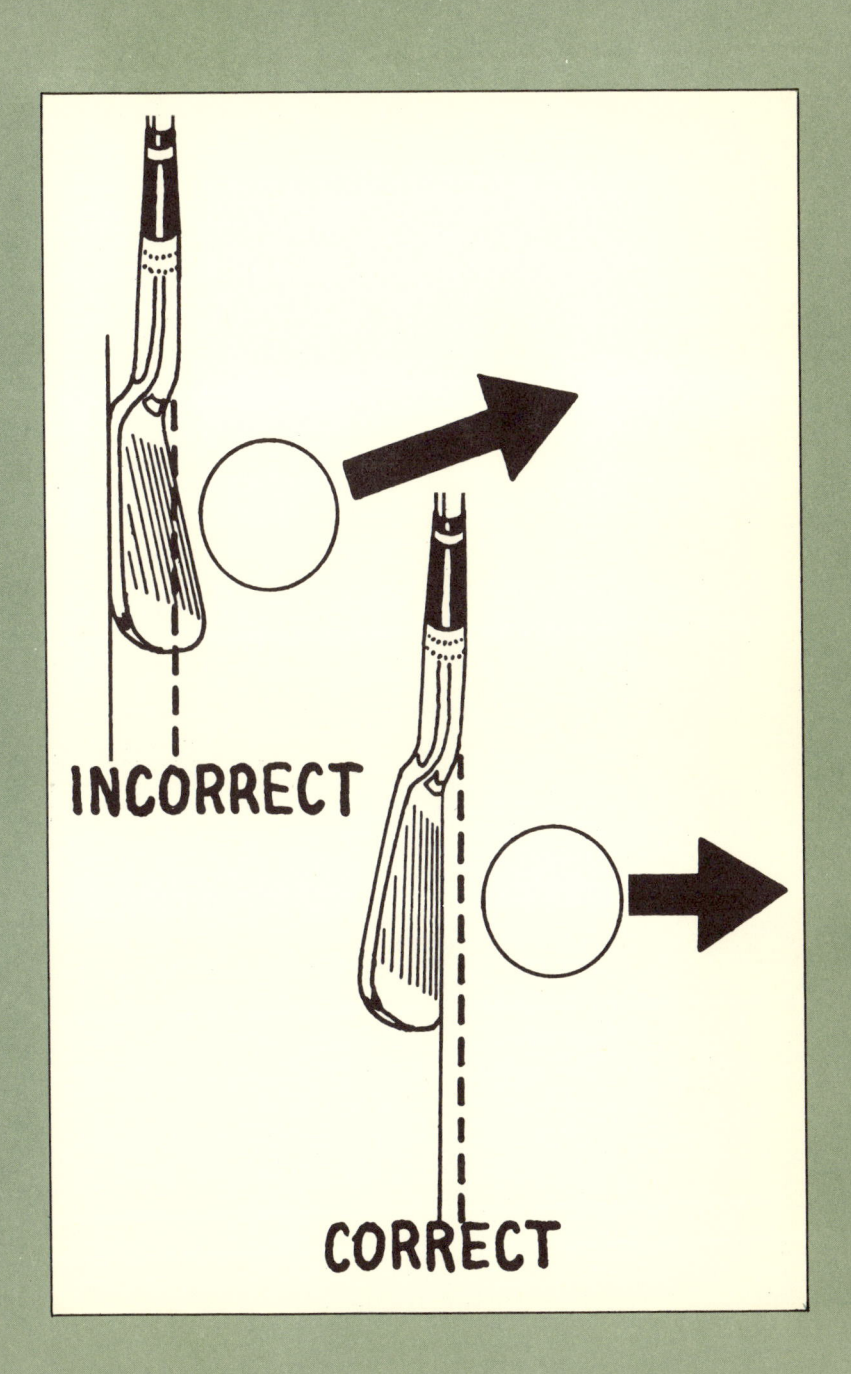

INCORRECT

CORRECT

When the ball is above your feet, control becomes especially important. If you hold the club as you usually do, you will be too far away from the ball for an effective swing. It's best to choke down on the grip; the more severe the slope, the farther down you should choke on the club.

Set yourself up to the right of the target, for the ball tends to hook or pull from this kind of lie. Your knees don't need as much flex as usual, for you have to stand tall to get a proper perspective of this shot. But keep your knees "easy."

With your shortened grip, it's a good idea to consciously limit your backswing for this shot. Be especially sure that you don't turn your wrist over—counterclockwise—at impact or you may get a bad hook. Swing the back of your left hand right at the target.

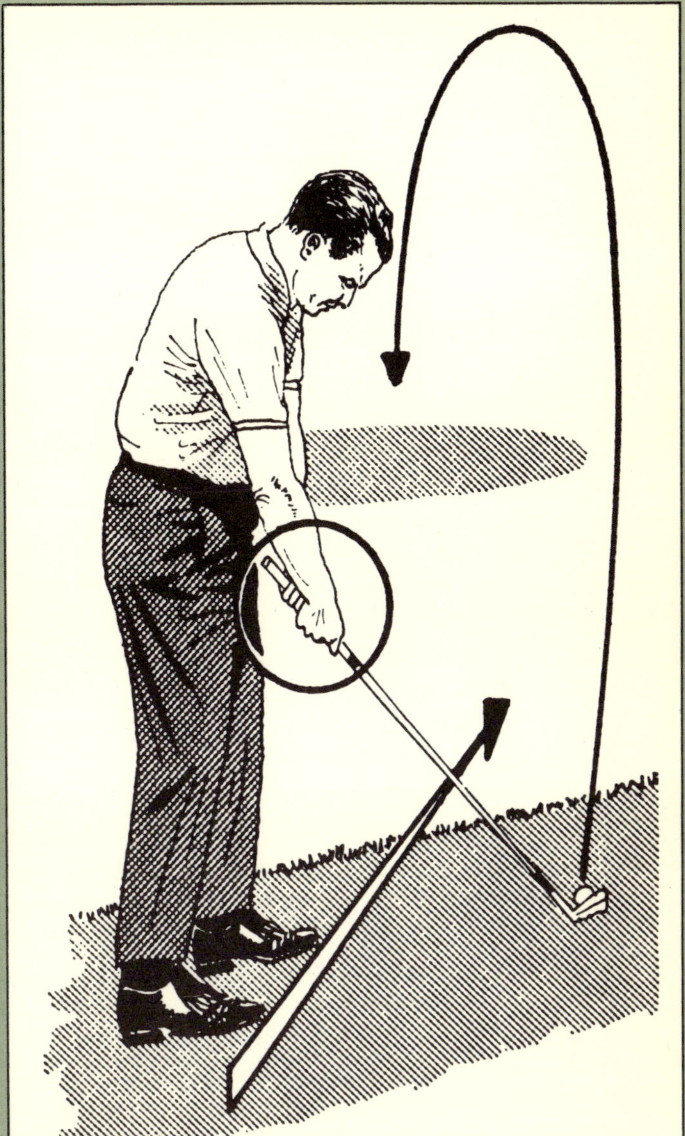

The big problem on shots from downhill lies is staying down on the shot. That is, swinging the clubhead through the ball in a downward arc which will get the ball well into the air. Whenever you set yourself up for this shot, think of this and determine to swing the clubhead in that manner.

A couple of other things—the ball will fly to the right, so aim to the left of your target; to help catch the ball on a downward arc, play it in the center, or slightly back of center, in your stance. At address, level your hips as much as possible by bending your right knee more than your left. Use a club you're confident will get the ball flying. As you swing back, be sure to move your weight to the right. If you leave it to the left, you may swing over the top of the ball and top it.

Above all, stay down on this one and try to move your clubhead along the contour of the ground for as long as possible after impact.

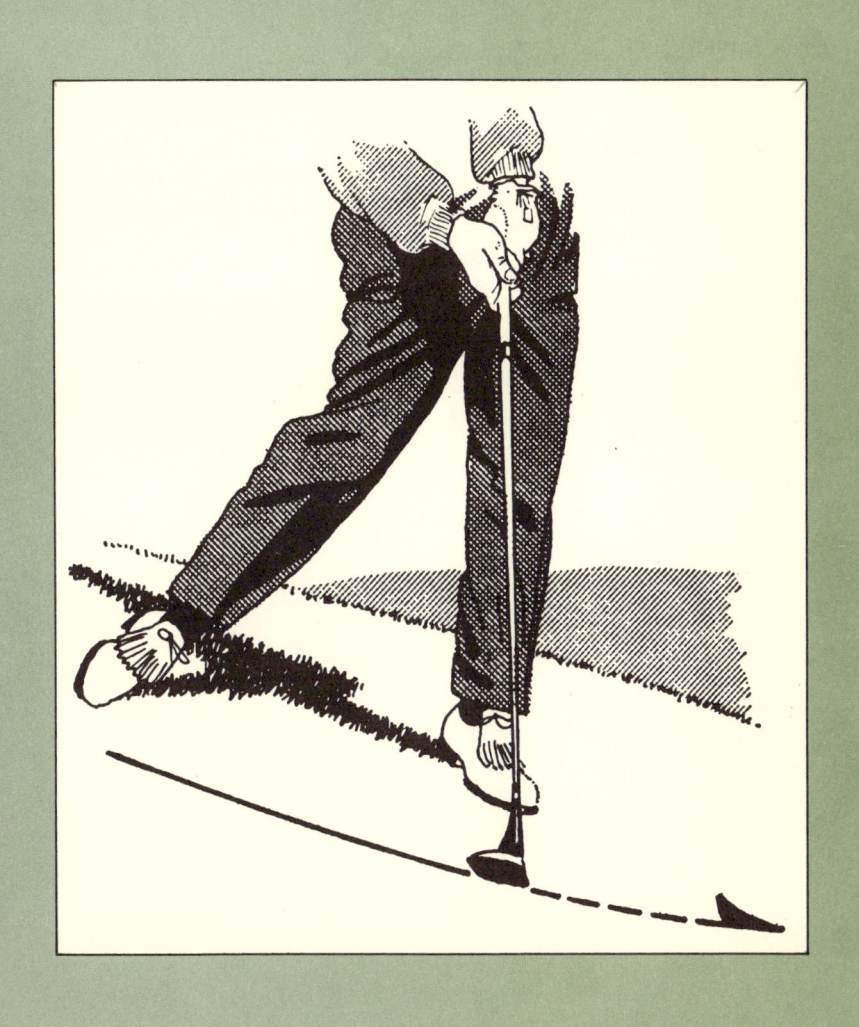

On longer shots, from the driver on to the long irons, backspin helps and steadies ball flight. When you get into shorter shots, it also is the reason approaches stop quickly after they hit the green.

To get good backspin on the shorter shots, "weld" the ball against the clubface at impact. On a good shot, the ball will be struck at a point just below the vertical center of the clubface, then climb up a fraction as the swing continues. That starts it backspinning.

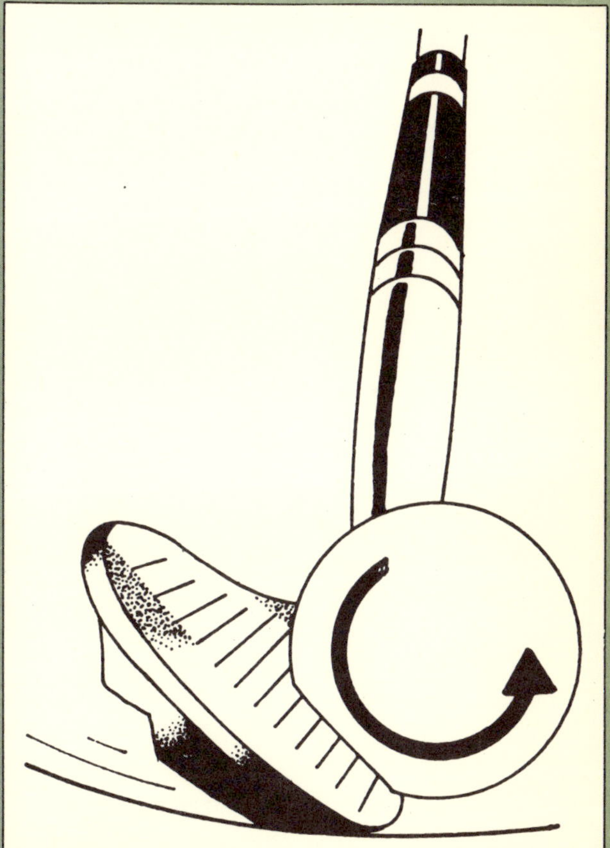

From all except the lightest rough, the clubface should be opened at address. Irons should be opened more than woods. When the club must travel through grass to get to the ball, the face will nearly always close somewhat at impact. That's because the grass grabs at the hosel and slows it down, while the toe of the clubhead swings around to close the face. Starting with an open face will counteract this and will help achieve higher, straighter shots from the rough.

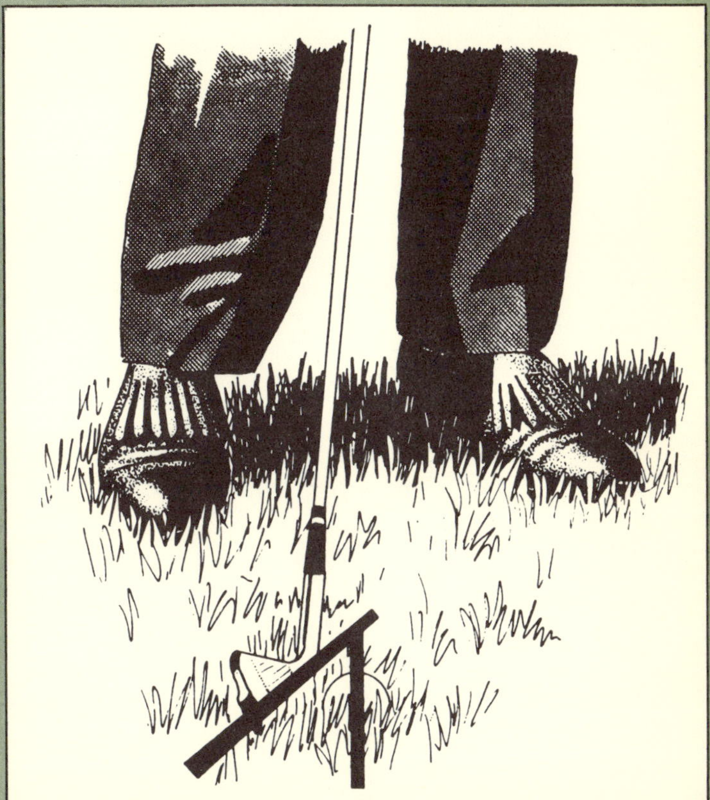

Knowing where to aim on every shot can overcome quite a few swing deficiencies.

A good rule of thumb is to plan every shot so that the next one will be easiest. Aim for a level place in the fairway; go for the spot that will give you the safest approach to the green.

On the illustrated hole, the 410-yard 6th at the Champions Golf Club in Houston, for example, the best tee shot would leave the golfer an approach over neither the pond nor the sand trap near the green.

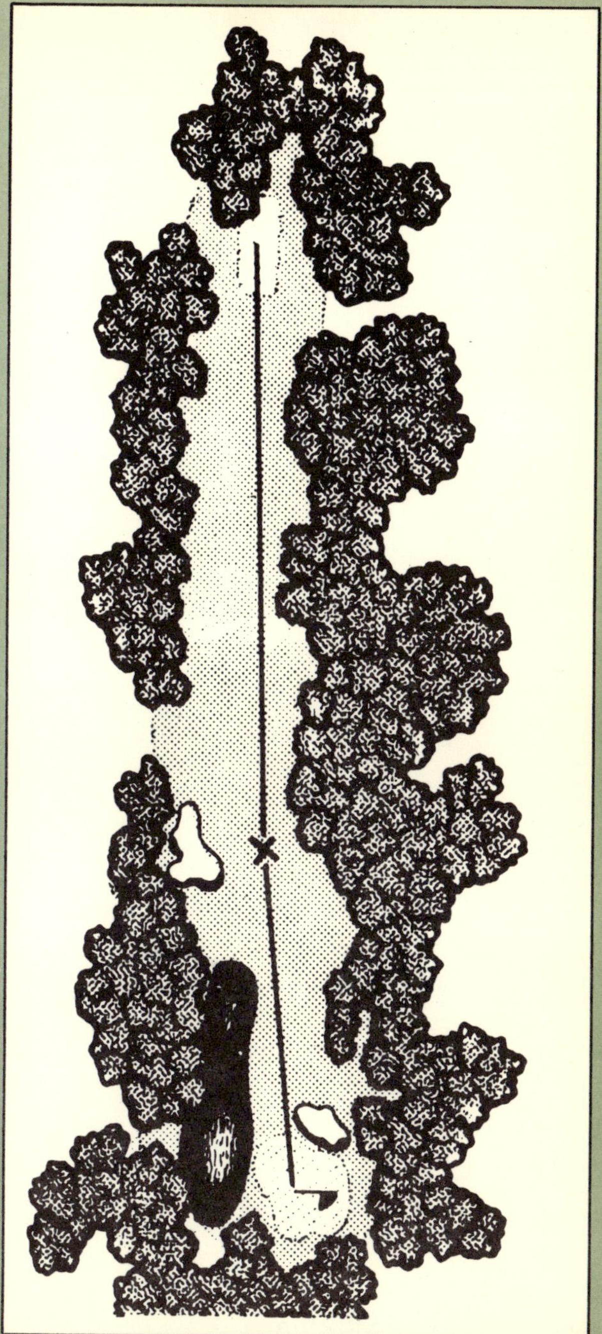

To loft the ball, play the ball more forward, toward the target, than usual, at address. Keep your hands behind the ball. Open the clubface, so that it faces to the right of your intended line. The ball will probably fade a bit from left to right, so take this into account when you are lining up. Open your stance, so that a line across the toes points left of the target.

Swing the clubhead back low and then as upright as possible. You'll want to sweep the ball up in an outside-in clubhead path at impact, as illustrated. Imagine this before you start your backswing and you'll likely get a good, high shot.

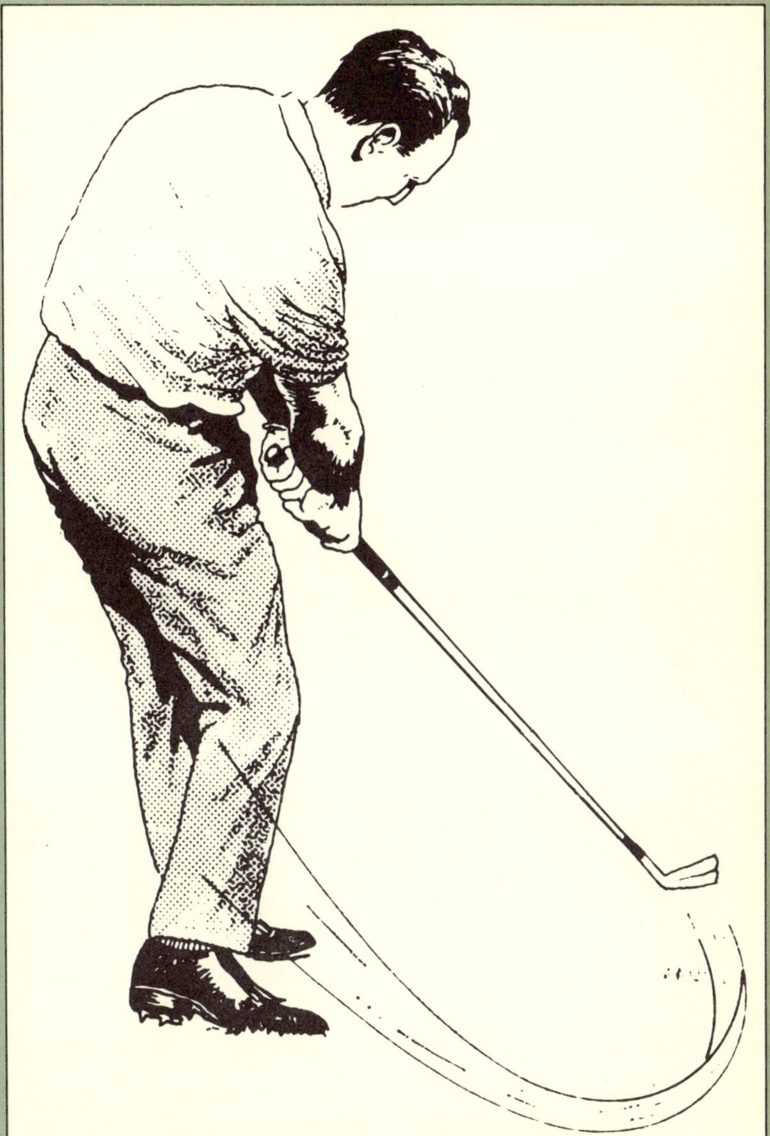

When the proper downward stroke is made with any iron, the clubhead will take a divot in front of the ball's original position. The sequence is the clubface striking the ball first, then moving downward for a bit past the ball and taking the divot at that time, as illustrated.

With this kind of impact the clubface squeezes the ball against the turf, imparting maximum backspin and producing the straightest shots. When you take a divot, you will get surprising distance as well as accuracy with less effort than a "sweep" would require.

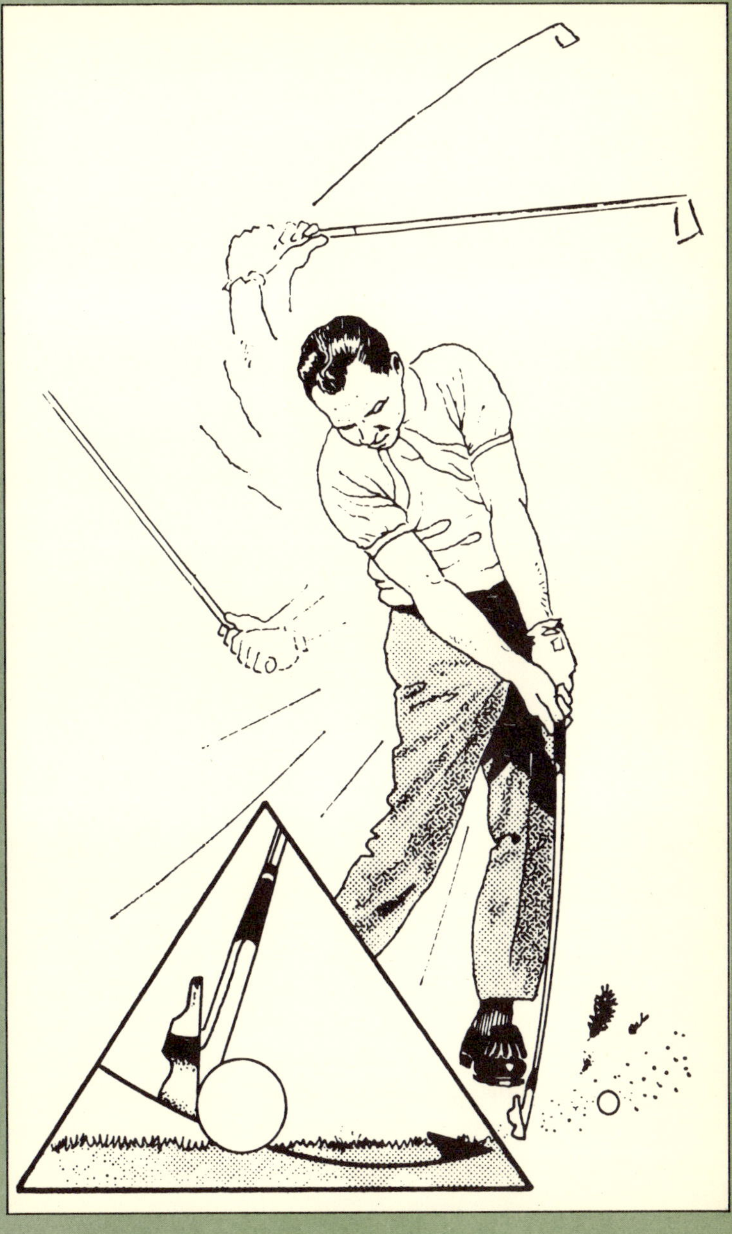

When the ball rests close to the ground in sparse grass, you have a "tight" lie. Unless the ball is deep in a divot hole or almost buried by higher grass, there is no need to alter your swing technique very much.

If you feel better, play the ball a bit more toward the center of your stance than usual. This puts your hands a little more ahead of the ball. Don't overdo this, though, or you won't get height on your shot.

Take your usual swing, but concentrate on making solid contact with the ball. Stay down on the shot at and after impact.

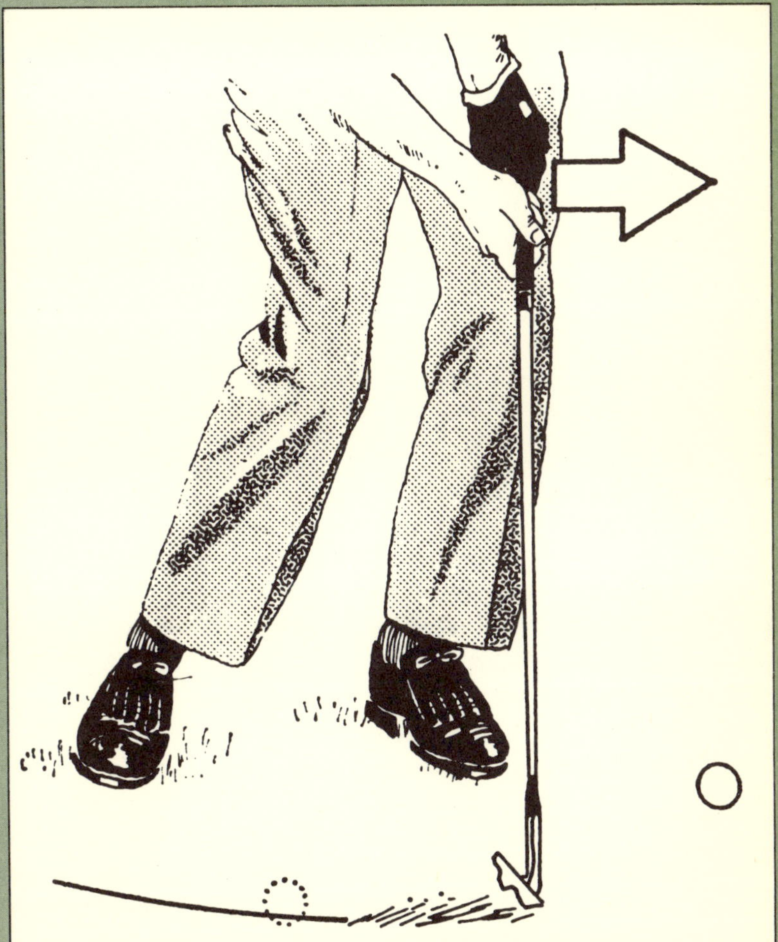

With short irons, you would be better off to choke down an inch or so on the grip and use one stronger club than you think might cover the distance—a 7-iron instead of a 6, for instance.

For these clubs (the 7, 8 and 9), play the ball a couple of inches inside the left heel. Don't open your stance excessively or you risk fading. Bring the clubface powerfully into the ball, pinching it against the ground. After a good shot, you'll discover you've taken a good divot from in front of the ball's original position, a divot aimed directly at the target.

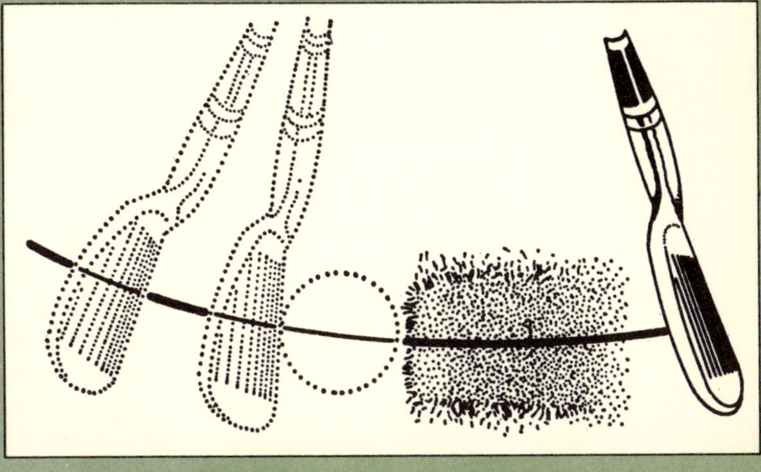

The high, soft, cut shot over a bunker and to a green is one you will face often in your golfing.

Using a fairway wedge, position your hands behind the ball at address. The ball is played forward, off the left heel, in a slightly open stance (left foot withdrawn more than the right from the intended line). This positioning increases the effective loft of the clubface.

Move your hands a quarter-turn to the left. This helps prevent a wrist-turnover at impact, and thereby helps get the ball well up. Swing with the feeling that you are slipping the clubhead directly under the ball, without any wrist-turn. You should take a divot in front of the original ball position.

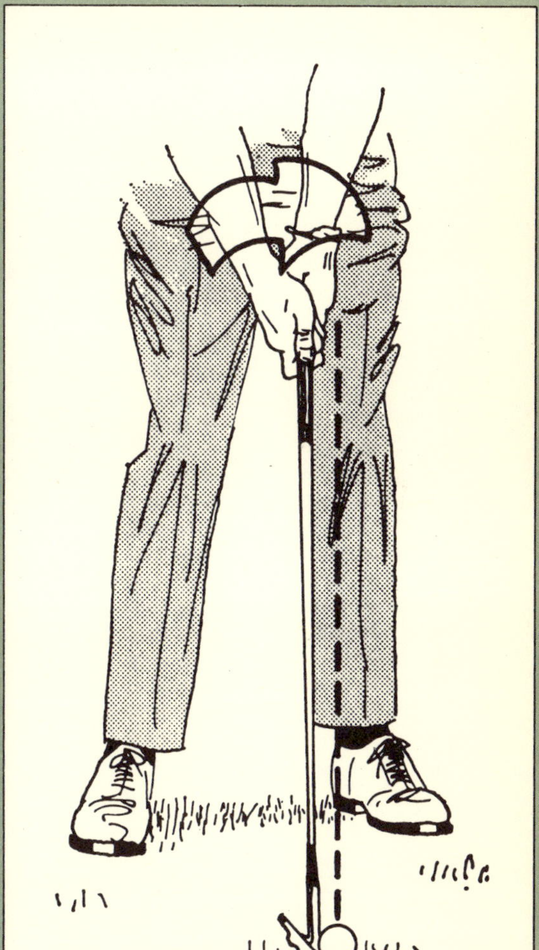

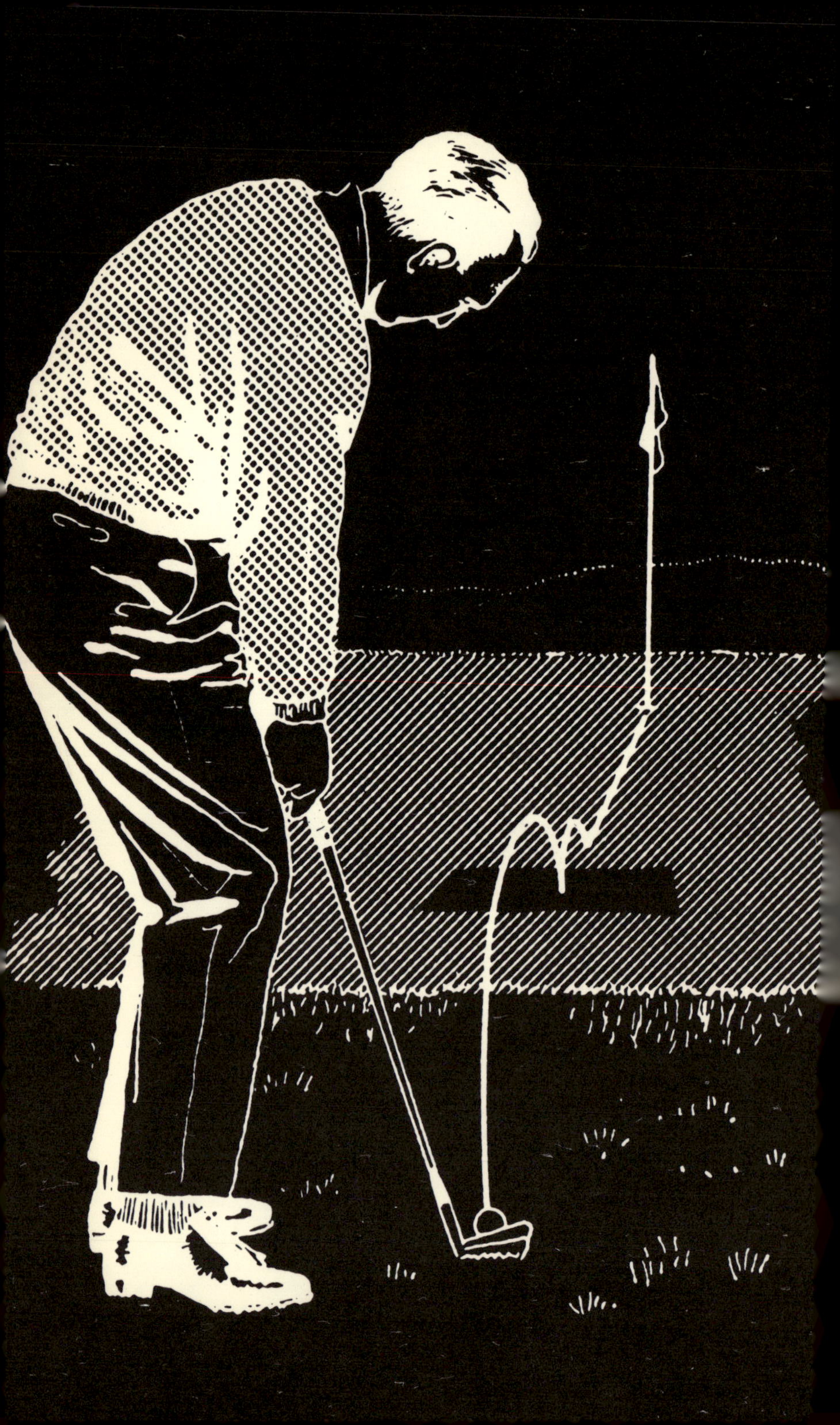

Around the Green

I am an advocate of the chip-and-run shot when the ball is just off the green. I like to get the ball onto the green fast and with the least area of chance. Because the aprons around the greens on most modern American courses are well-manicured, many pros prefer to putt from just off the edge. Others like to punch the ball toward the hole, giving it more loft and letting it bite into the turf.

In 1949, Sam Snead, playing the 71st hole at the Medinah Club near Chicago in the U. S. Open Championship, attempted to putt the ball from the heavy grass on the fringe. He muffed the shot and blew the championship. The bite shot requires excellent technique. Only the golfer with experience can master it.

The chip-and-run is a product brought over from the British courses where traditionally the apron is tough and wiry, the green rock-hard from lack of irrigation. Through necessity, the British have learned to play the shot very well. A similar shot—a pitch from farther off the green—has been developed in the arid Southwest and has been popularized as the "Texas wedge."

For my chip-and-run shot, I use a No. 5 or a No. 6 iron, without too much loft. I study the terrain, roll of the green and so forth and pick a spot where I want the ball to land, figuring how much roll is needed from that spot to reach the hole. I give the ball a firm rap. I try not to roll it past the hole.

For week-end golfers, I would recommend that they spend fifteen or twenty minutes before a round practicing on their chip shots. They should place the ball in tough positions and see how close they can get to the hole. This pre-round maneuver will help them develop feel and confidence.

The idea is to get down in two. After the chip, unless the ball rolls into the hole, there is still the putt. In modern golf, putting has become the name of the game, although I consider all facets as highly important.

Nevertheless, it is common knowledge that in this age of brute strength, there is little to choose among the top tournament golfers from tee to green. All of them hit with prodigious power. Most of them are so strong that they can recover from most rough without a severe penalty. They play to the greens with such precision that they all resemble machines. Most observers concede that tournaments are won and lost around the greens. The next time you read of a player winning a tournament, note how many birdie putts he made during the round.

Around the Green

Use the pitch-and-run shot when you are shooting to a very hard green, one that will not hold a normal approach. This would be especially true if you were also shooting with the wind coming from behind you. Such a shot could also be used when it becomes necessary to shoot under intervening tree limbs. Of course, there should be no hazards between your position and the green.

To hit the low shot that will run after it touches down, play the ball toward the right foot. This puts your hands ahead of the ball and lessens the effective loft of the clubface. Be certain that the face is pointed directly at the target.

Swing back as low as possible and don't use too long a backswing. Come into the ball low, also, with your hands well ahead of the clubhead. Keep the clubface square to the target as long as possible after impact. The finish may be shortened.

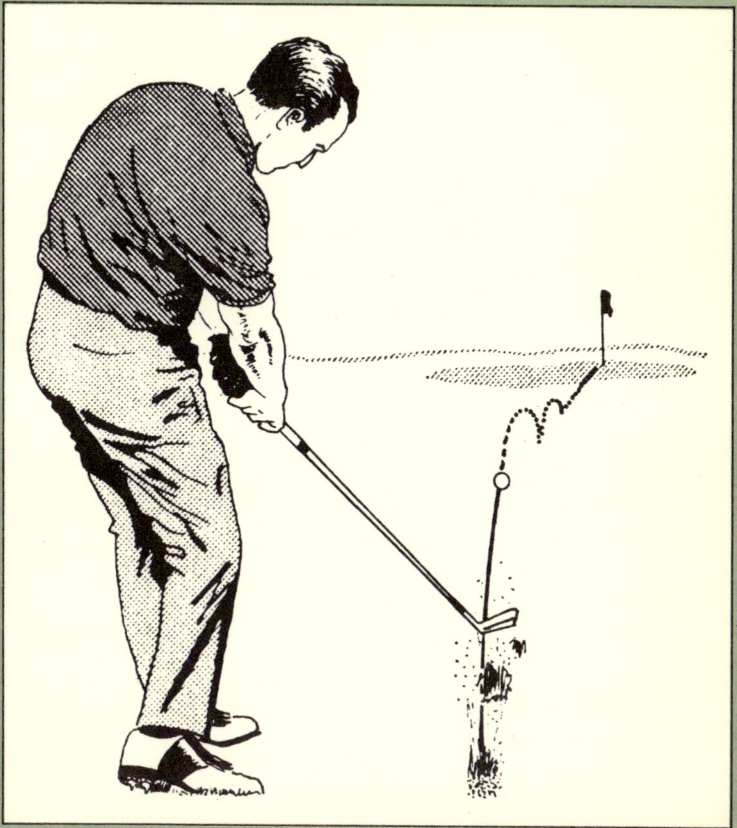

I like to chip almost exclusively with my arms and shoulders, although, of course, the body must move a little to keep everything fluid.

For the normal chip, my stance is narrow and slightly open, left foot withdrawn more than the right from the intended line. I like to play the ball back of center. The ball can then roll readily when it lands on the green.

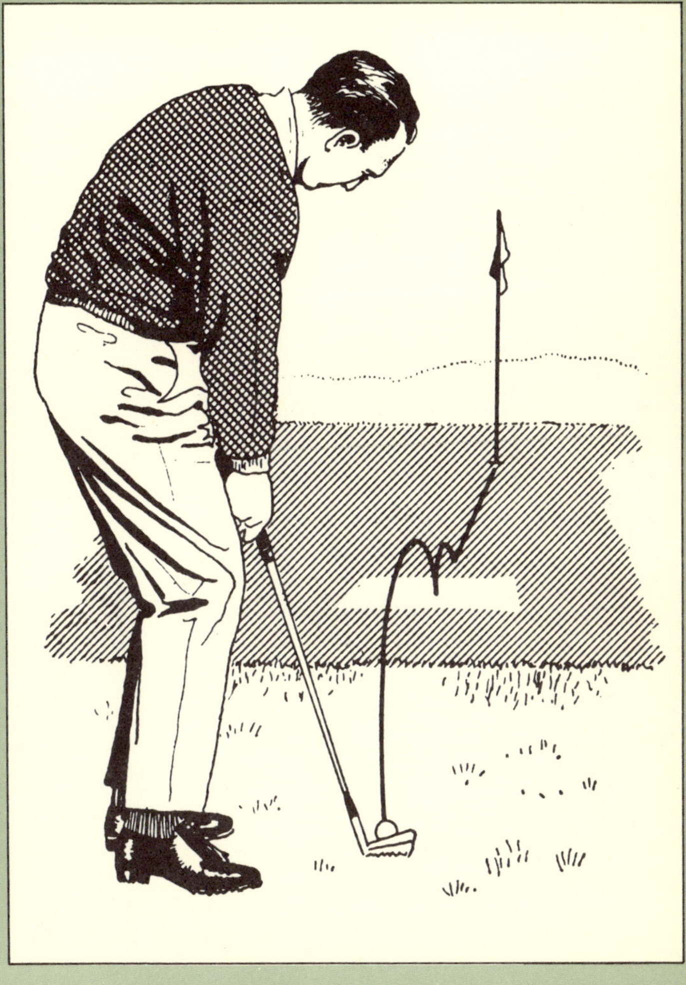

Whenever possible try to hit a chip so that it rolls the last two-thirds of the distance to be covered.

To accomplish this, use a club with the least amount of loft that will allow you to land the ball on the green. The closer you are to the green, the lower-lofted should be the club.

Pick a spot on the green where you want the ball to land, then imagine the swing force that will get your shot to that point. Swing the clubhead back low without too much wrist-break and accelerate it into the ball.

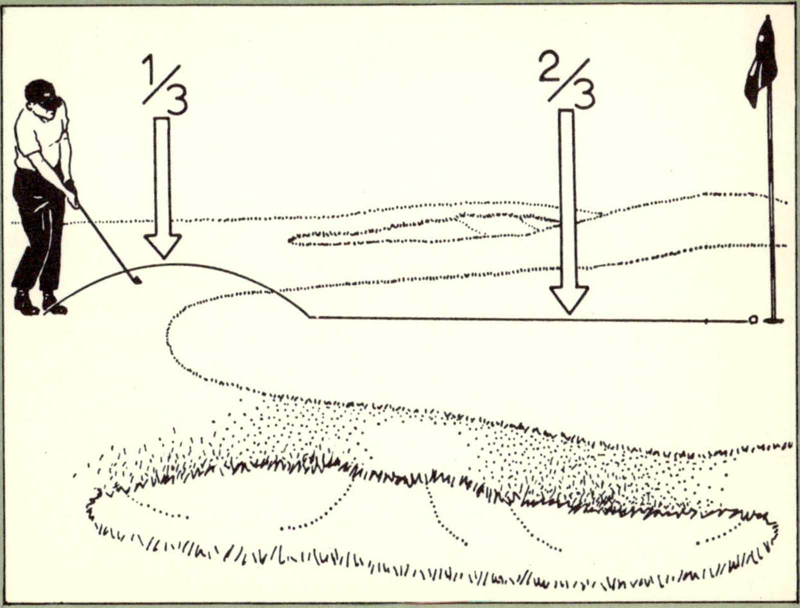

1/3
2/3

Before every chip shot, plan just how you want your shot to go. Once this plan is set in your mind, you will find the shot's execution that much easier.

Good chippers use the club with the least amount of loft that will get the ball onto the green. That is, they use straighter-faced clubs near the green's edge, but those with more loft from farther out. A low-trajectory shot is best, for it will run more readily and with less chance for sideways bounces.

Don't make your target too small, or you may be nervous about hitting it.

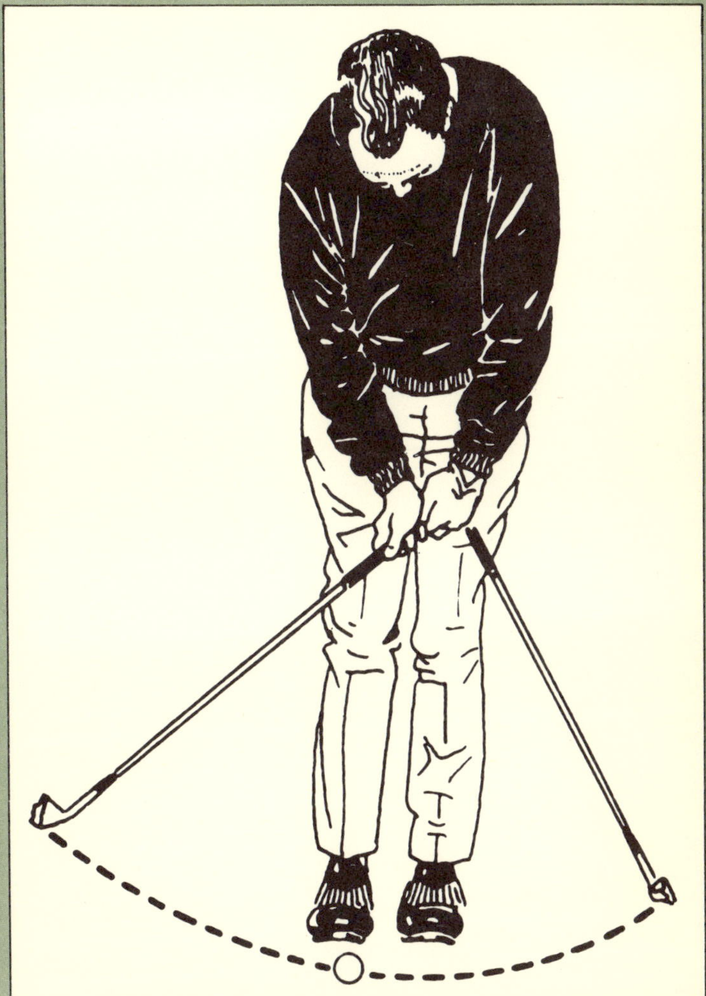

Approach shots to the green from uphill lies will fly higher and fall shorter than normal, so you should choose one or two clubs "more" (e. g., a 5-iron instead of a 6-iron) than you would usually use for the distance required.

The steeper the hill, the more toward the target you should play the ball in your stance. Level your hips and shoulders by bending the left knee in toward the ball at address. Aim to the left of your target, for this shot tends to fade from left to right.

Swing the clubhead back low. Don't transfer too much weight right on the backswing or it may stay there on the downswing. Really hit the ball hard.

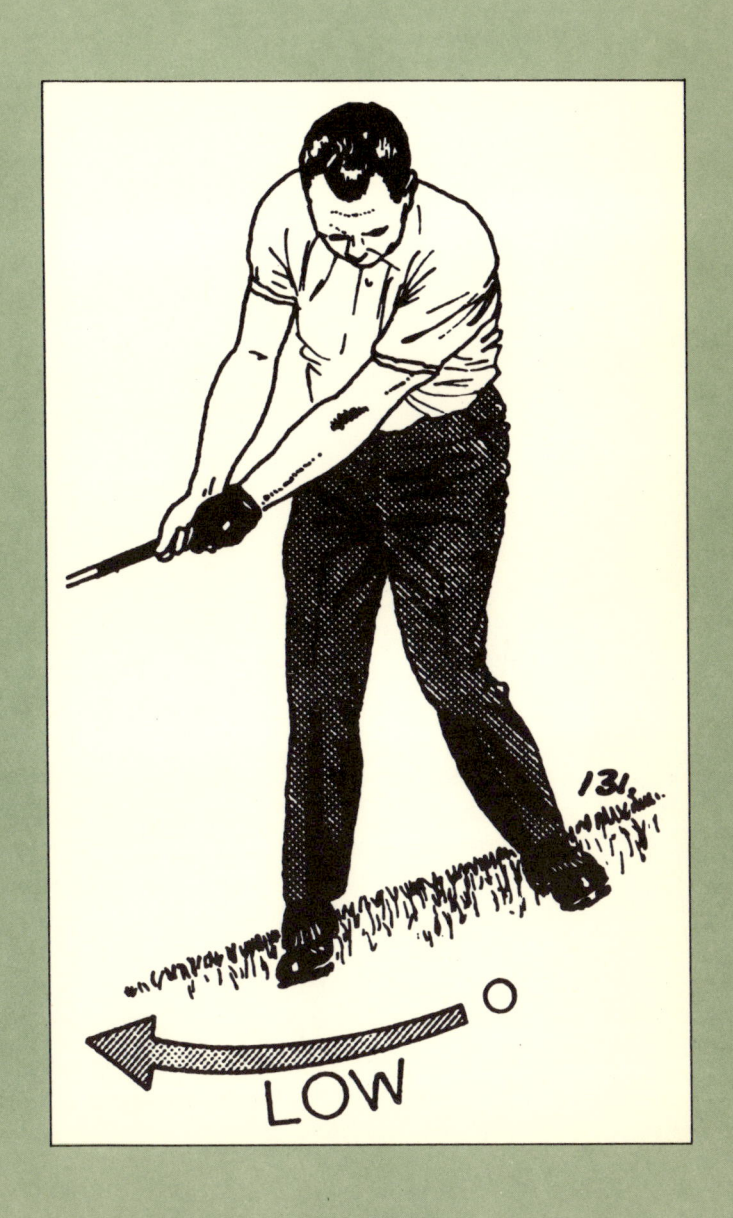

LOW

You can expect a low shot from a bare lie, so if you are hitting to a green, plan to hit the run-up shot. The idea is to land the ball in front of the green and let it run on.

Play the ball in the center of your stance and position your hands ahead of the ball at address. This, in effect, hoods the clubface, tilting it forward a bit, and reducing the loft. It's a good idea to shorten your grip on the club.

Take a shorter-than-usual backswing and try to clip the ball off the ground, taking little divot. Hit the ball first, for if the clubhead hits the ground before impact, it will bounce up and you'll probably skull the ball.

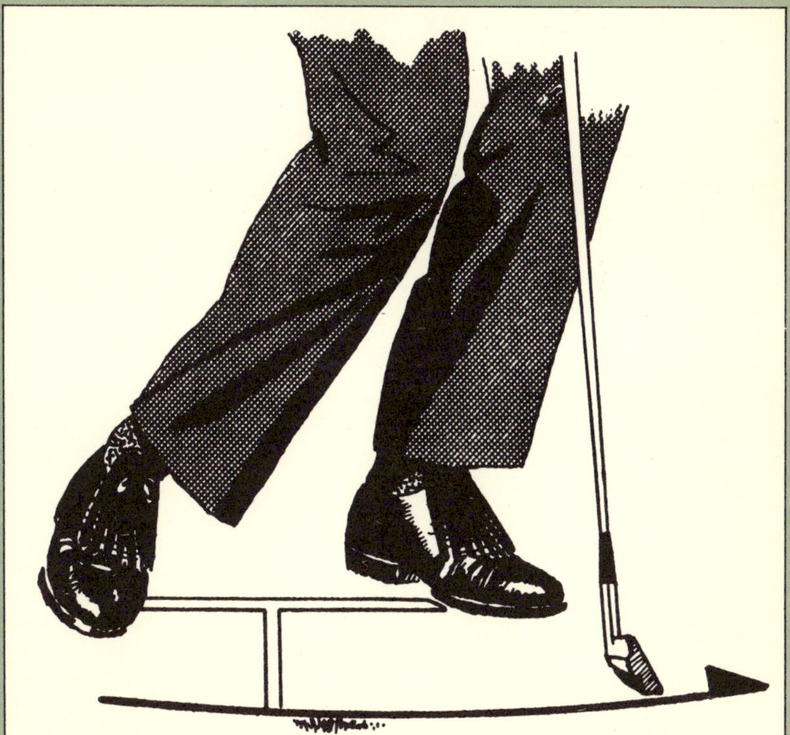

The full backspin shot can be hit best from firm turf and close-cropped grass, and from no closer than 100 yards. Use a narrow square stance (feet rather close together, both equidistant from the intended line). Play the ball in the back half of your stance, toward the right foot. Keep your weight to the left as you swing, and come down abruptly on the ball, as illustrated. The sharp downward stroke will impart maximum backspin to the shot.

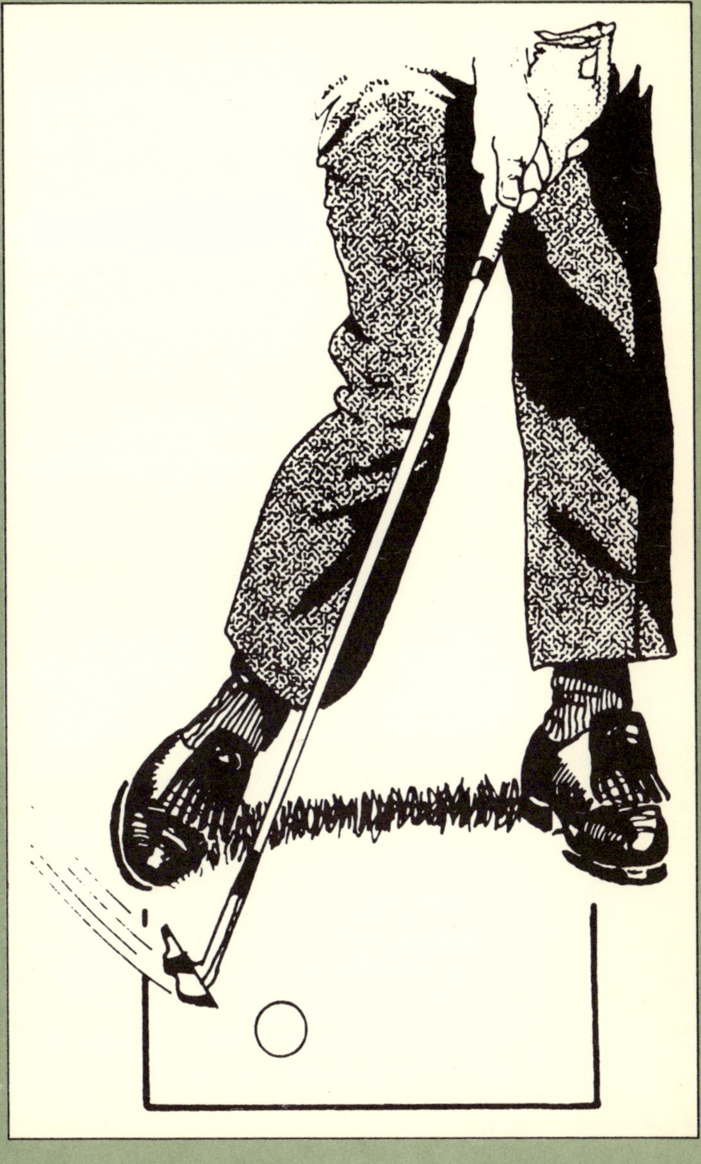

Never play the ball too far back in the stance for the ordinary fairway wedge shot. If you do, the hands get too far ahead of the ball at address, and you'll hit a low ball.

The proper wedge positioning is to play the ball perhaps two inches inside, or behind, the left heel, with the hands only slightly ahead of the ball. The stance should be opened, but not too much. Place the turned-out left foot so that the toe is about an inch or so farther away from the intended line than the right foot.

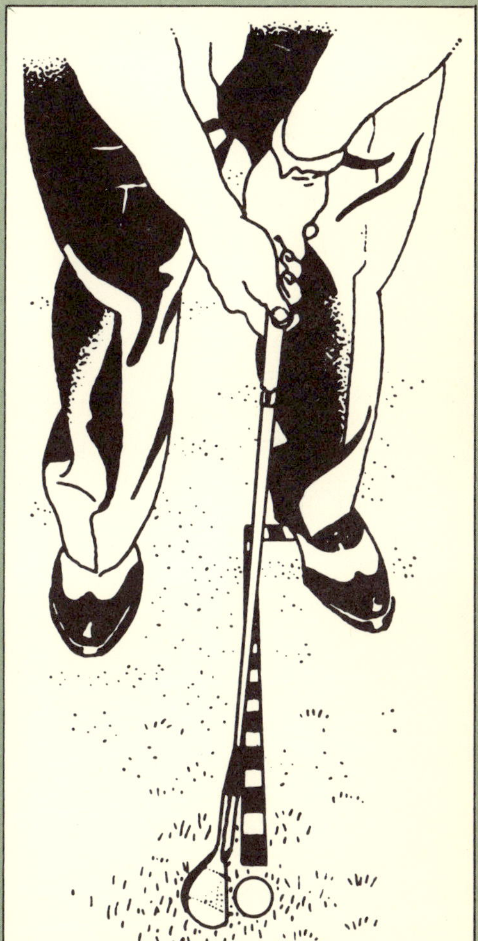

Shooting Out of the Sand

Foot and body position is important on all golf shots, including those from sand. It makes the correct swing that much easier to execute.

From normal sand (not packed hard, wet or very soft), the idea is to swing the clubhead through the sand underneath the ball. The clubhead never touches the ball. The force of it moving through the sand will pop the ball out. The arc of the swing is best described as a very wide "U," flattened out on the bottom.

Play the ball off the left heel with a very open and narrow stance. Your hands should be slightly behind the ball, a factor which "lays back" the clubface, giving it additional loft. Plan to strike the sand with the face "looking" at the pin about two inches behind the ball. The face should not turn over at impact, so maintain a firm lefthand grip. Then be sure to hit through—don't stop at impact with the sand.

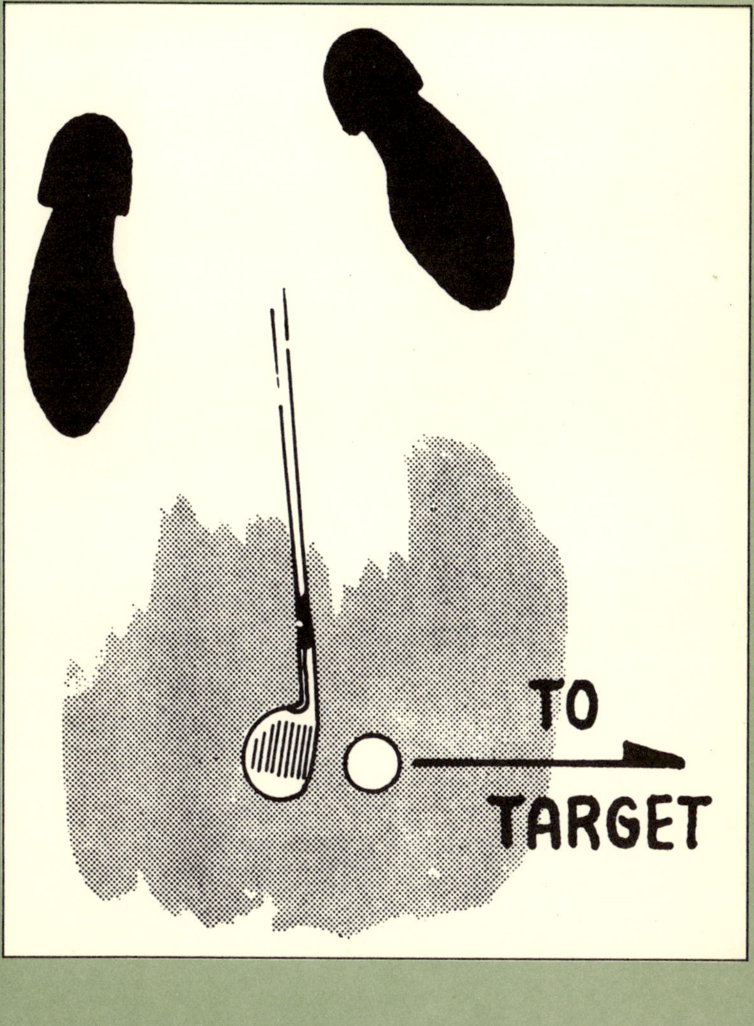
TO
TARGET

One of golf's more troublesome shots is from a buried lie in the sand. To get the ball out and flying, you must swing so that the sand wedge clubhead digs deeply into the sand from a point very close to the ball.

At address, turn the face in so that it looks to the left of the target and keep your hands well ahead of the ball. This helps to counteract the reverse turn of the clubhead at impact with the sand.

The backswing and downswing are steeper than normal, so break your wrists early as you take the club back. Swing down directly at a spot only a fraction of an inch behind the ball. Your grip must be firm to withstand the resistance of the sand. Don't leave the clubhead in the sand—it must be swung on through.

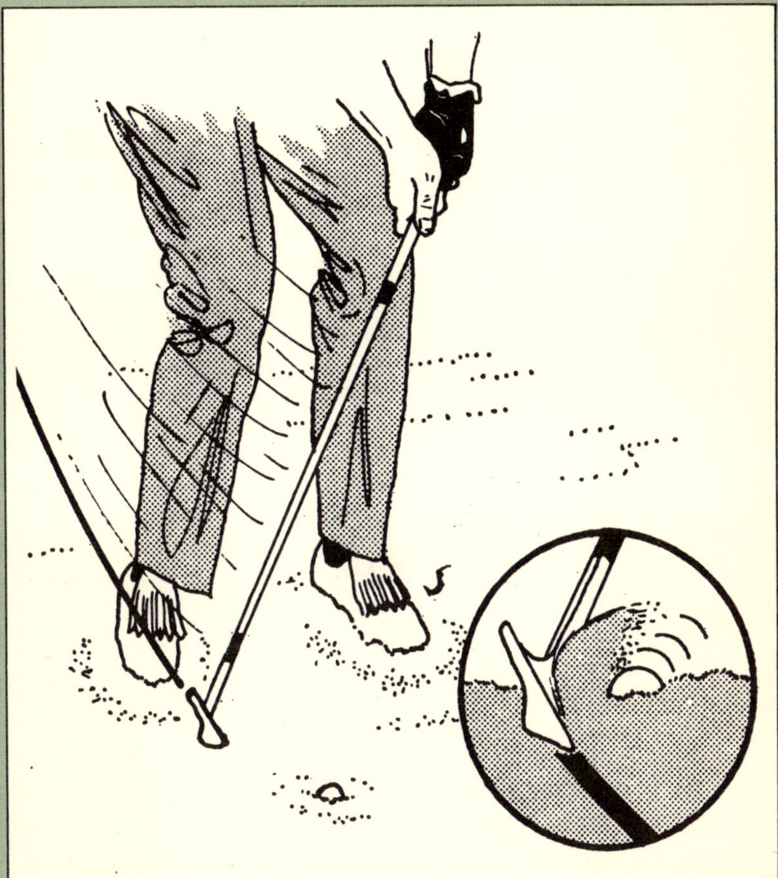

In the sand shot, the clubhead should enter the sand about two inches behind the ball. The clubhead then sweeps under the ball and comes out on the other side of its original position. The force, or pressure, of the clubhead moving through the sand pops the ball up and out of the trap and to the green.

Continue your swing on through the sand to a full finish. If you hesitate at impact you are likely to merely bury the clubface and not get the ball out of the trap.

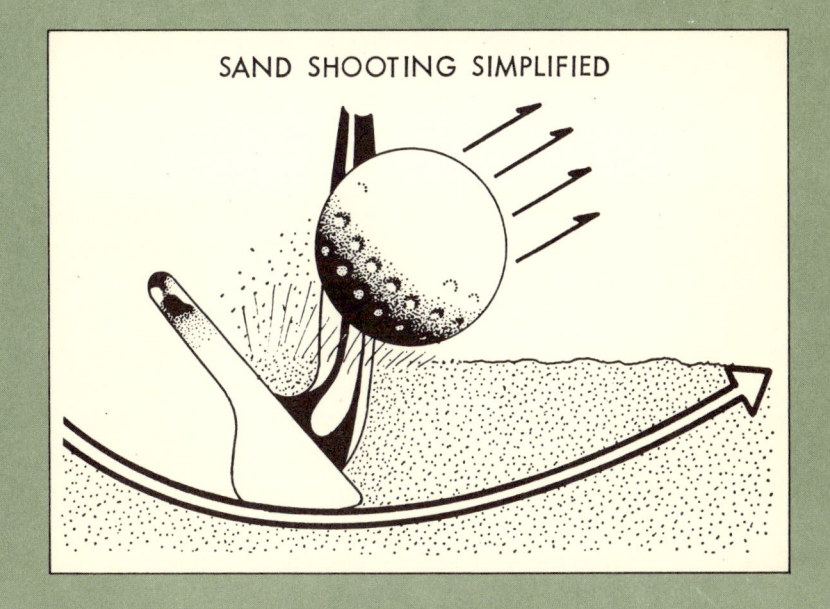

SAND SHOOTING SIMPLIFIED

Knowing where to aim for the sand wedge to enter normal sand in various lies is an important part of the sand bunker battle.

1. For the level lie, the clubhead should enter the sand about one inch behind the ball.

2. For the uphill lie, the clubhead should enter the sand as close as possible to the ball. If the lie is extremely uphill, try to hit the ball and sand at the same time.

3. For the downhill lie, the clubhead should enter the sand about two inches behind the ball and at a very abrupt, or steep, angle.

NORMAL - 1 inch

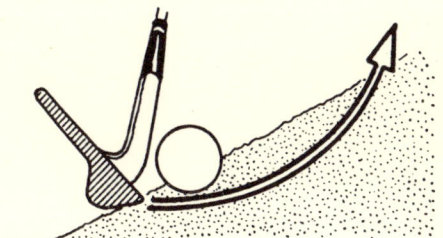

UPHILL - less than 1 inch

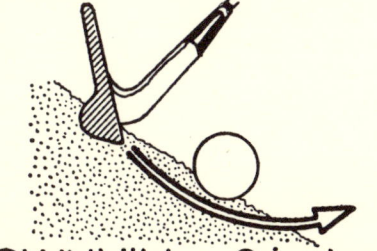

DOWNHILL - 2 inches or more

When sand-shooting, the idea is to skin a slice of sand out from under the ball. The clubhead never hits the ball.

Take an open stance (left foot withdrawn more than the right from the intended line) and position your hands behind the ball—away from the target—at address. Then you'll more likely hit the sand about two inches behind the ball when you swing.

Also, weaken your grip by placing your left hand more on the side of the club and your right more on top than normal.

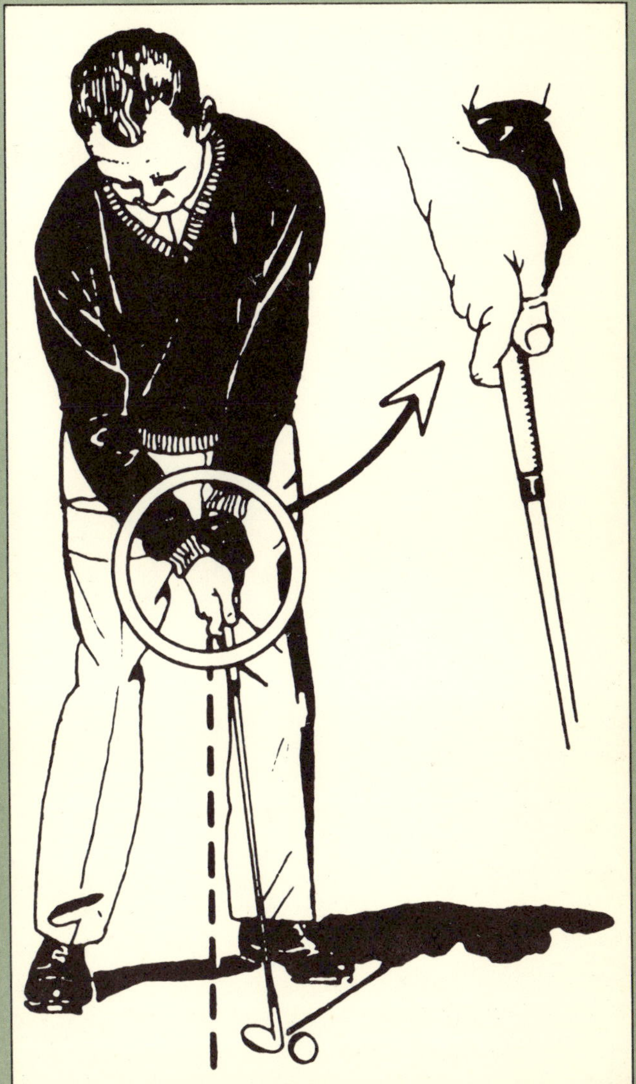

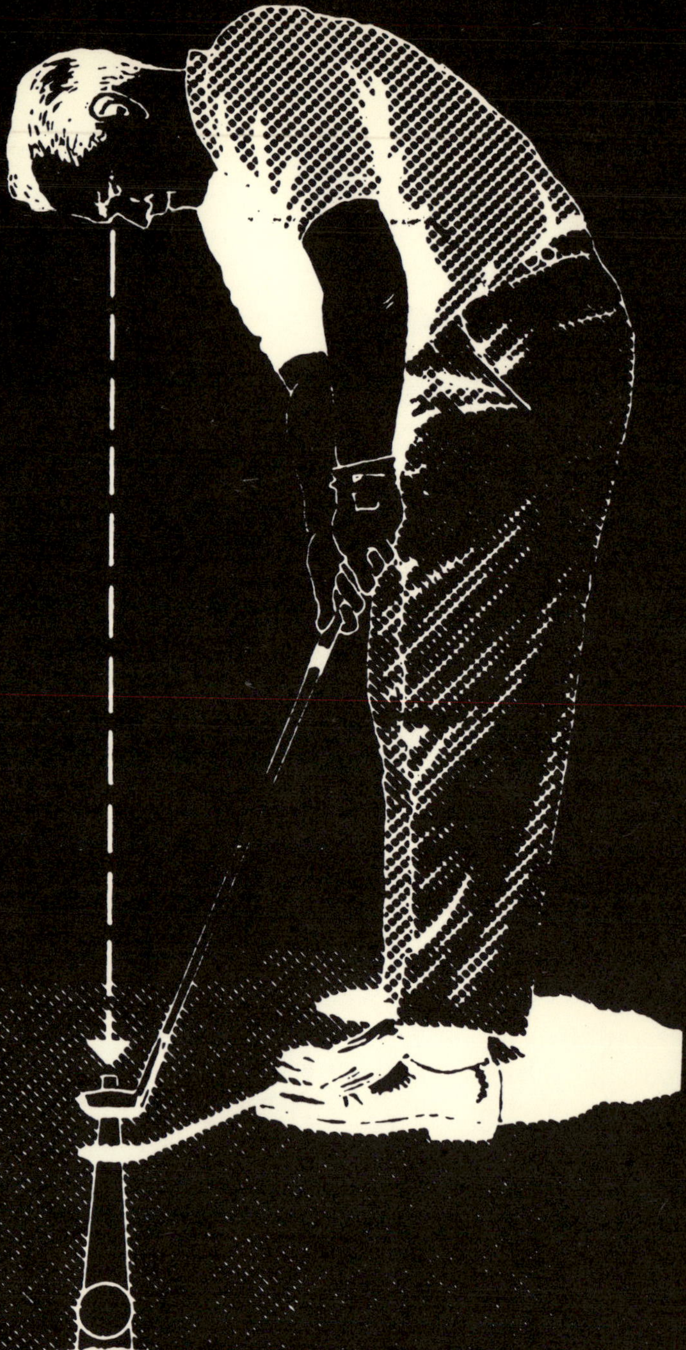

On the Green

To many people who follow golf, whatever success I have achieved as a tournament professional can be traced to my putting. I am constantly reading—much to my surprise and often chagrin—what a great performer I am on the greens. Take the putting blade out of my hands, some have said, and I would be just another golfer. I am amazed that the legend has lived so long.

I am quite aware how this legend was born. I don't know how I will ever be able to correct it, although I personally feel that my game from tee to green is far superior to my short game, particularly as it involves putting. I think there are numerous better putters on the tour. On the other hand, I am quite proud of the way my all-around game has stood up under the pressurized test of big-time competition.

In 1959, I played in the U. S. Open Championship at the Winged Foot Golf Club in Mamaroneck, New York. Few Easterners knew who I was. Ben Hogan was shooting for his fifth Open title. Sam Snead still swung the club with the grace of a tree swaying in the wind. And a young man named Arnold Palmer, winner of the 1958 Masters, was captivating galleries.

On the first day of the tournament I shot a 71 and used only 28 putts. The next day I had a 68 with only 30 putts and at 139 I had a one stroke lead over Hogan and Palmer, tied at 140. But nobody was greatly impressed. I was just a jolly fat man—I weighed 212 at the time but I didn't consider myself very jolly—with a good putting stroke.

People began taking more serious notice when I used only 27 putts on the storm-marked third round for a 69 that gave me a three-stroke lead. I almost lost my lead on the final day after suffering a bee sting, but I held on to take the title with a 282. It was recorded that I had a total of only 114 putts for the four rounds. From then on, I was Billy Casper, the putter.

Actually, it was putting that gave me the worst problems in my early years as a pro. I worked on my putting to the point that I finally felt I knew my way around on the greens. It's true I got to be a fairly good putter—no sensational one—and enjoyed some wonderful sprees in occasional tournaments, such as the 1959 Open. In recent years, I have been offended that so much emphasis has been placed on my putting to the detriment of the rest of my game.

Not that I do not consider putting important. It is most important. As a matter of fact, 50 per cent of a golfer's strokes are taken on or around the greens. I think the ideal way to teach golf would be to start the beginner on the putting green, teaching him the fundamentals, then move to chipping, pitching and finally driving, in that order. This is the reverse of the normal procedure, which is to start with the drive and work down to the putting.

I don't think enough time is devoted to the short game, particularly in the case of the new golfer. If a man wants to become a good golfer, it is essential that he learn this gentle art around the green. Greater attention should be given to chipping and putting practice. It's the bigger part of the game in miniature. The stroke is the same. You can hook a putt as easily as you can hook a drive.

A point which all of us would be wise to remember is that an extra stroke around the green counts the same as one lost because of a wild drive or poor judgment on playing the approach shot to the green. You would be surprised how many strokes can be saved, how much your scoring could be improved, by improving this short game touch through more diligent practice. Few men are able to stand on a tee and bomb a ball 300 yards as Nicklaus can. Anyone can learn to chip and putt.

The Test of Nerve

Putting is an individual art. There is no basic formula for the way you grip a club, place your feet or swing the club. Golfers agree on a few vital points such as keeping the putting blade square to the line or trying to use an unhurried stroke and rapping the ball firmly—but general techniques are as varied as the color of the golfers' slacks.

I use the reverse overlapping grip, holding the putter in my right hand with the index finger of my left hand overlapping between the second and third fingers of my right hand. This grip, with variations, is used by most of the pros. Yet some have success with the double overlap, the baseball grip and the cross-handed grip. I stand square to the line, my feet about twelve inches apart, with my head directly over the ball.

I don't recommend that anyone copy my particular style or, for that matter, anyone's particular style of putting. You must adopt a stance, a grip and a feel that is comfortable for you. The key to good putting is comfort and confidence. If it gives you any satisfaction, remember that a frail, 110-pound girl may putt as well as a big, rugged man.

Just as technique should be left to the individual golfer, so should the selection of type of putter. Pro golfers are notorious for experimenting with putters. I daresay that most top players have dozens in their workshops and they're always willing to try one more if their touch should go sour. There are blade putters, mallet-heads, goose-necks and hickory-shafts. Find one you like and practice with it. No one yet has discovered a miracle blade.

The only advice I would dare give anyone on the problem of putting would relate to preparation and general philosophy. To be a good putter, you must learn to read the terrain—the grain, the break, the various undulations—and you must concentrate. I have known good putters who put themselves into a sort of trance and visualize the ball dropping into the hole.

The success or failure of a putt is determined on the first six inches of the ball's roll. This is the making or breaking point. This sets the line. The blade should be kept low, square to the line, then brought back smoothly and without rush. You should rap the ball firmly. Remember, if the ball spins off the low side of the cup—the so-called amateur side—it means that you didn't give the ball a chance.

On the mental side, many golfers have trouble with their putting because they "freeze" on the green. For some reason, putting has become the supreme test of a golfer's nerves. These nerves become frayed with time. The sport is saturated with the names of great golfers who, in advancing years, were able still to strike the ball beautifully from tee to green only to lose their confidence on the greens.

The average golfer finds even greater fear in the sand bunkers. Once a golfer sees a shot fly into a trap, he is stricken with panic. His poise disappears. He is sure he won't be able to get out for two weeks. The fear is misplaced. Many top pros have become so adept at blasting out of the sand that in many cases they prefer, if they miss a green, to land in a bunker rather than a patch of knotty rough somewhere in the same vicinity.

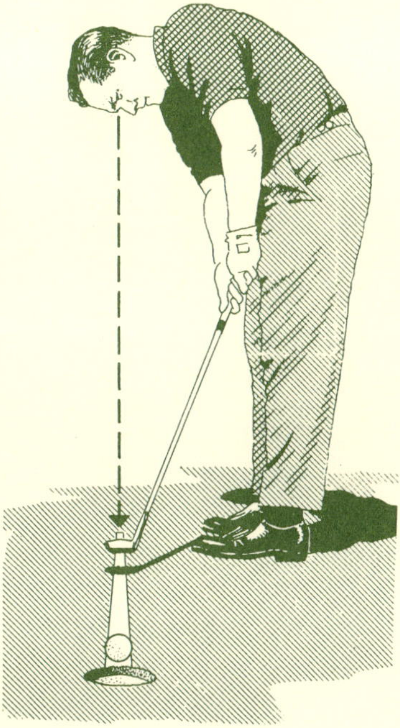

On the Green

If there is one basic fundamental to putting, it's the immovable head. Those who keep a rock-solid head throughout the putting stroke are usually good putters.

Of course you should not concentrate so hard on this that you tighten your neck muscles. This would set up a certain tenseness in the rest of your body that would interfere with a smooth swing. Instead, before every putt determine to look directly down on the ball until impact, then at the ball's original position until you hear it fall in the cup or know that it has stopped.

The steady head will do wonders because it serves to keep the body from swaying, and thereby helps prevent clubface-ball impacts, and missed putts.

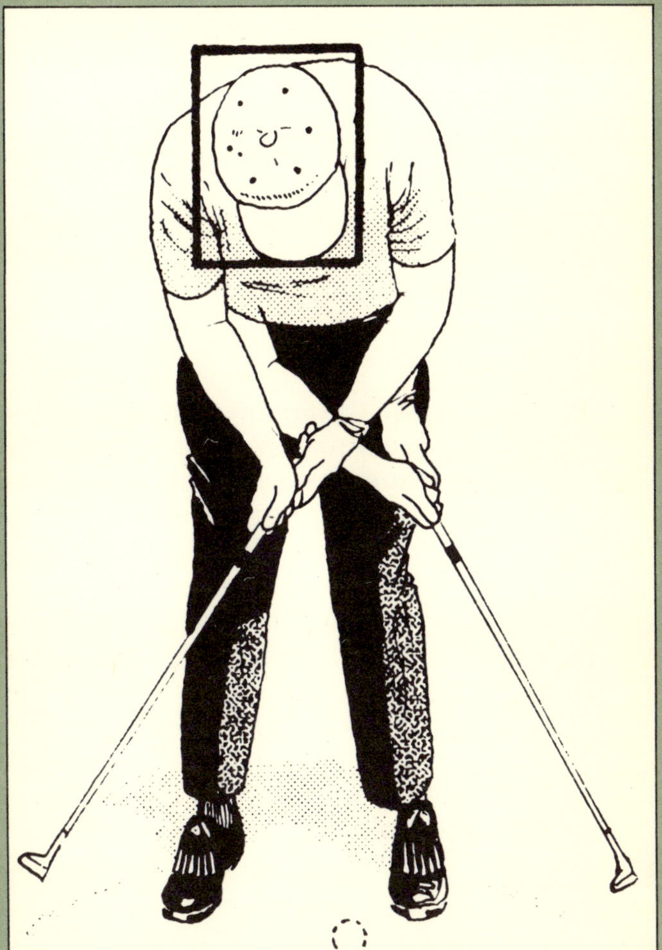

Most putts are missed because of a half-hearted stroke at the ball. Every putt should be made positively, that is, with firm hands, solid impact and enough speed to hold the ball on the intended line. On all but the tiniest of putts, the clubhead should move well past the ball's original position after impact.

I like to think that I am holding the clubface in position with my left hand and striking the ball with my right. Take the clubhead back with the left hand, and keep it low to the grass. Don't let that left hand turn in any direction. On the downswing, be sure to accelerate into and past the ball. Think of your right hand as providing the impetus. Never, never look up until the ball has stopped rolling.

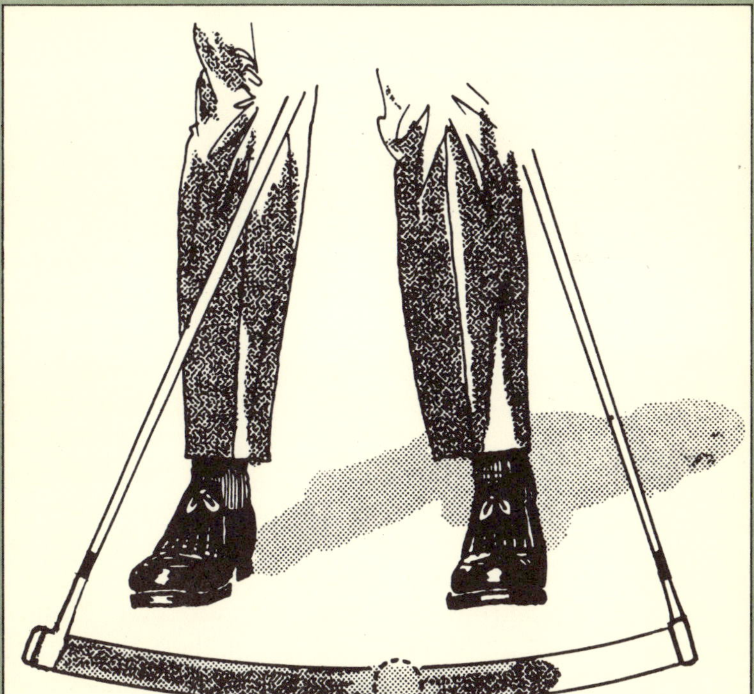

Half-heartedness has no place in putting. Good putters are quietly determined to get that ball into the hole This determination—maybe confidence is a word you prefer—has quite a bit to do with how a golfer swings his putter.

Hesitation will most often show its face on those short mind-burners, three feet or less. Have you picked the right line? If you feel doubts, you may slow your stroke at impact. Such putts will easily wobble off-line.

Choose your line, then live or die with it. Putt with confidence; if you do, you'll accelerate the clubhead into and past the ball without hesitation. This acceleration is important on all putts, long or short, but it's those little ones you must be most careful about.

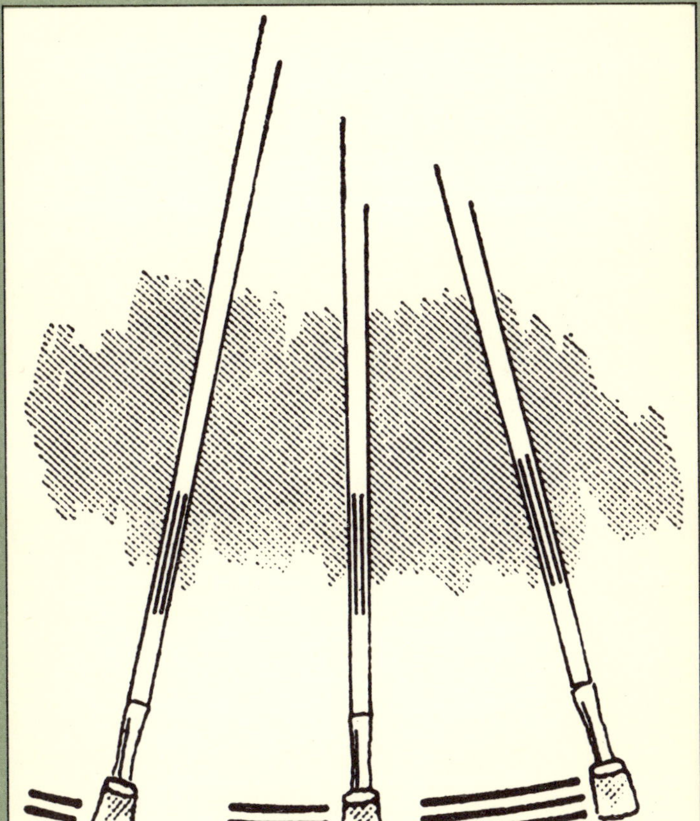

In the illustration, note that my shoulders and hips have not turned away from a line exactly parallel to the initial line of the putt. In my style, I allow my right wrist to break freely on the backswing. The left wrist breaks down and under. I do not turn or rotate my hands on the backswing, which would bring the clubhead back too far inside the intended line.

But what's more important, my head and upper body have not budged away from the target in the backswing nor will they move in the other direction on the downswing.

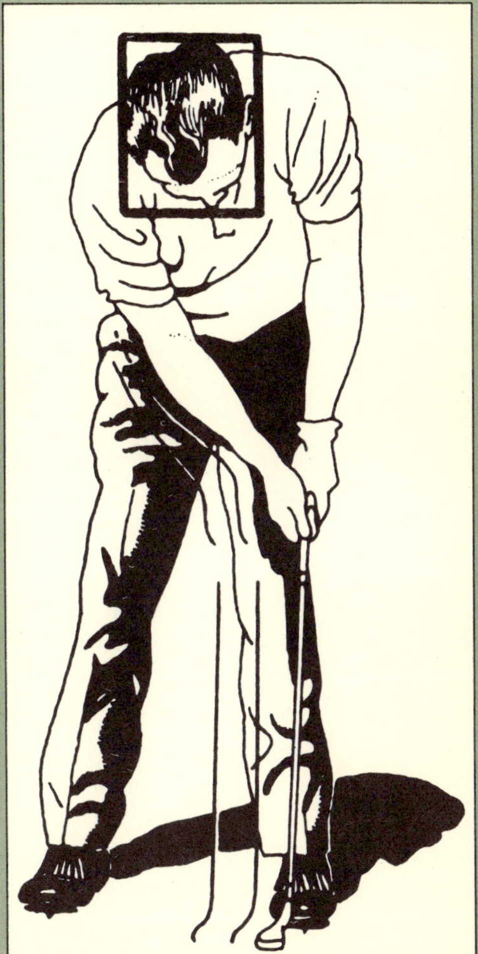

Golfers who miss most of their putts to the left, especially the longer ones, are probably allowing the left wrist to break too soon at and after impact.

A good way to check yourself is to take a look at your post-impact position in putting. The back of your left wrist should still be pointing down the putting target line after you hit the ball (see illustration). If you have allowed your left wrist to break, you've flipped the clubhead at the ball and probably closed the face at impact.

Use whatever wristbreak is comfortable for you on the backswing, but minimize it at and after impact for the straightest putts.

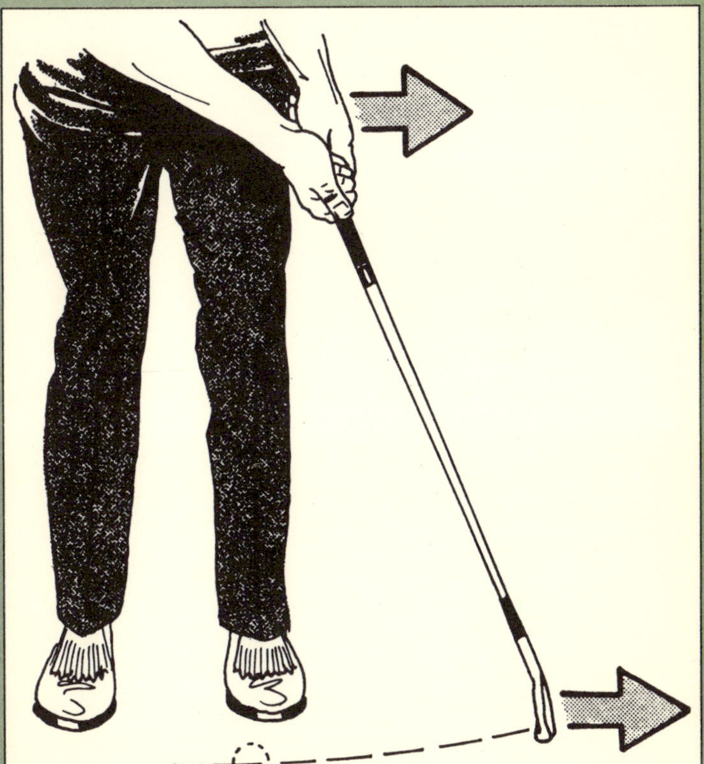

On northern courses, the grain of the grass has a minimal effect on putting. That is because the bent grass used on such greens is often cut so closely, there simply isn't any grain left.

However, if the greens are a little "shaggy" or if you're putting on Bermuda grass greens found in warmer climates, it's wise to pay some attention to grain.

If the grass looks shiny from behind the ball, you know that the grain is with you and the ball will run more easily. If the sheen is dark, then the grain's against you, and you will have to be bolder. If you can't tell anything from behind the ball, take a look from the side. A cross-grain running uphill will hold a sidehill putt on line; if it's running downhill, the break will be more noticeable.

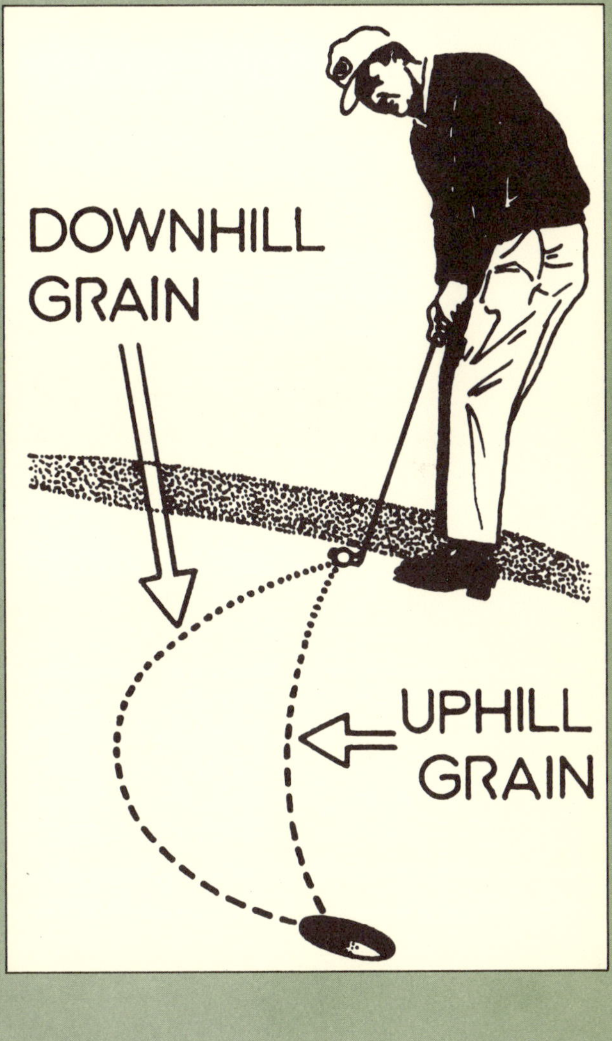
DOWNHILL
GRAIN
UPHILL
GRAIN

Putting is the most sensitive part of golf. Most of the errors that hurt a golfer's putting are mental.

The anxious putter will start moving his head toward the target somewhere around impact. He might be so anxious that he wouldn't be looking at the ball when he hits it. Needless to say, this will throw any putt off-line.

A steady head is most important in putting. So concentrate on the ball. Look down on top of it as directly as you can at address. On short putts, especially, never look up until the ball has stopped rolling—you'll find it rattling most of the time.

It's surprising how many putting errors this will cure.

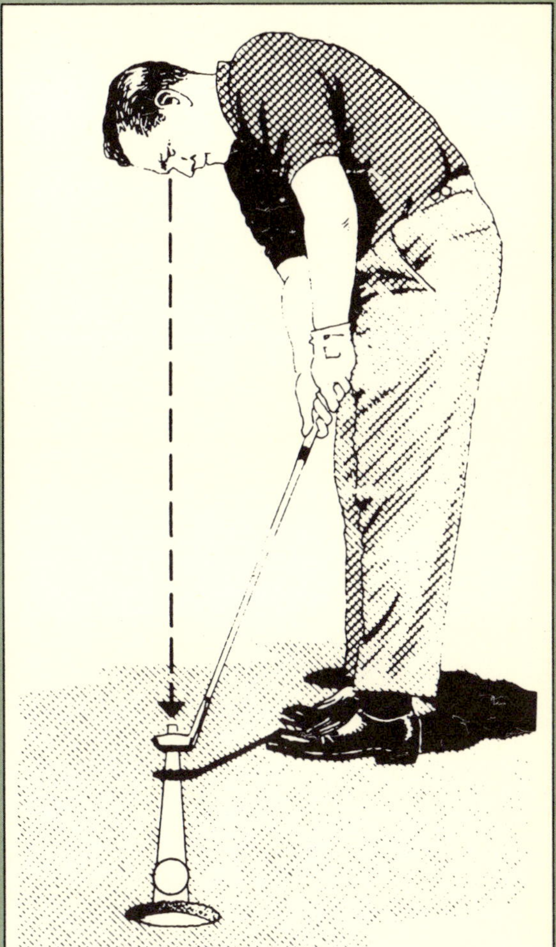

Billy Casper—Career Highlights

TOURNAMENTS WON:

1956
Labatt Open

1957
Phoenix Open
Kentucky Derby Open

1958
Bing Crosby National
Greater New Orleans Open
Buick Open
Brazilian Open
Havana Invitational

1959
U.S. Open
Brazilian Open
Portland Open
Mobile Sertoma Open
Lafayette Open

1960
Portland Open
Hesperia Open
Orange County Open

1961
Portland Open

1962
Doral Open
Greater Greensboro Open
500 Festival Open
Bakersfield Open

1963
Bing Crosby National
Insurance City Open

1964
Doral Open
Colonial National
Seattle Open
Almaden Open

1965
Insurance City Open
Bob Hope Classic
Western Open
Sahara Invitational

1966
500 Festival Open
Western Open
U.S. Open
San Diego Open

1967
Canadian Open
Carling World Open

1968
Los Angeles Open
Colonial National
500 Festival Open
Greater Greensboro Open
Greater Hartford Open
Lucky International

1969
Bob Hope Desert Classic
Western Open
Alcan Golfer of the Year

Billy Casper—Career Highlights

Official Money Winnings

Year	Place	Official Winnings
1955	58th	$3,253.82
1956	12th	$18,733.41
1957	9th	$20,807.83
1958	2nd	$41,323.75
1959	4th	$33,899.39
1960	4th	$31,060.83
1961	4th	$37,766.78
1962	4th	$61,842.19
1963	11th	$32,726.19
1964	3rd	$90,653.08
1965	3rd	$99,931.90
1966	1st	$121,944.32
1967	3rd	$129,423.23
1968	1st	$205,168.67
1969	10th	$104,689.00

Special Awards

Leading Money Winner 1966, 1968
Player of the Year 1966, 1968
Vardon Trophy Winner 1960, 1963, 1965, 1966, 1968
Member, Ryder Cup Team 1961, 1963, 1965, 1967, 1969
Golf Writers of America—Pro of the Year Award 1968
Byron Nelson Award 1966, 1968
Putter of the Year Award, 1966, 1968
Honored by the Academy of Professional Sports 1967, 1968

About Billy Casper

It might seem strange that a diet consisting of such exotic foods as whale and bear meat and avocados could bring about a significant change in a professional athlete's career, but that is what appears to have happened to Billy Casper. In 1964 he consulted a Chicago specialist and discovered he had enough allergies to become the subject of a casebook. Fortunately, about the only things he was not allergic to were grass and golf balls. Up to that point he had established himself as one of the top performers on the tour. Over an eight-year span, he had won twenty-one events and earned more than $200,000. One of these victories was the 1959 U.S. Open. Then, along came that wild diet and Billy, fifty pounds lighter as a result, zoomed to still greater heights. Since then his victories, including his second U.S. Open in 1966, have pushed his earnings over the million-dollar mark. He is one of the fastest players on the tour and a master of self-control under pressure.